Jesus, the Man of Many Names

'The book is a real eye-opener. I really do believe I have been privileged to review an important book – an extraordinary tour de force. Unquestionably this book will make a massive contribution to current thinking about Jesus at a time when both his humanity and divinity are being questioned.'
Chris Hill, author, broadcaster and international Bible teacher

'Congratulations on a great book.. . . It is undoubtedly inspired by the Holy Spirit and written for such a time as this. Your explanation of Daniel is explosive, revealing the message hidden in all that coded language which for so long has cloaked many minds regarding the timing of future events, in particular the coming of the Messiah.'
Julia Fisher, author and broadcaster

'"In the beginning was the . . ." – finish this well-known phrase or saying without using the first verse of John's Gospel, using neither English nor New Testament Greek and by reference only to an Aramaic translation of the Hebrew Bible. Can't be done? This "voyage around our Father" – and His Son – will open your eyes in the best tradition of travel and exploration. Steve Maltz has a gift for combining pacy writing with crystal-clear distillation of his own careful study of scholarly resources and a firm grip on the Gospel. The result is a fascinating new landscape of insight – it's not so much Jewish roots of the Christian faith as "Jewish knowledge" of the Gospel. The Bible-believing reader need not fear any distraction from the Word of God, only reinforcement in some unexpected places. Enjoy!'
David Andrew, editor, Sword *magazine (formerly* Prophecy Today*)*

'*Jesus, the Man of Many Names* is in one sense unique. Steve Maltz has been able to bridge the gap between the scholar and the ordinary Christian, and turn scholarship into a life-giving encounter with a living person. Over many years I have read and studied the subject of the Jewishness of Jesus, as well as lecturing and writing about the subject. Reading *Jesus, the Man of Many Names* has been an inspiring experience, making the Jesus of the first century and the New Testament vibrant and real in a fresh way. Many Christians unfortunately have a vague and sometimes sentimental notion of "Christ" and "Jesus", and also completely misunderstand the background to the Jewish rejection of Jesus as Messiah. This book changes all that, and the more widely it is read the better. I strongly recommend it.'
Derek White, founder, Christian Friends of Israel UK

'I was and am most interested in your style and approach. As a writer you are most readable – humorous, leading the reader on, putting things in a contemporary and user-friendly way, and with a sense of infectious joy in your discoveries.'
Richard Harvey, Tutor in Hebrew Bible, Hebrew language and Jewish studies, All Nations Christian College

'I'm really enjoying it. I just love the way you make what can be quite complicated theology both accessible and fun. There is some stuff which I already know but it's presented in a way which makes it enjoyable and really good revision.'
Kit Eglinton, web consultant and counsellor

'Written at great cost. So many veils are lifted in this book.'
Norma Gregory MBE

'Anyone with a desire to explore the mysteries of Scriptures and meet the totally Jewish Messiah of whom they speak will love this book.'

Michele Guinness, writer and speaker

Jesus, the Man of Many Names

A fresh understanding, from the dawn of
time to the end of days

Steve Maltz

Authentic

MILTON KEYNES ● COLORADO SPRINGS ● HYDERABAD

13 12 11 10 09 08 07   7 6 5 4 3 2 1

First published in 2007 by Authentic Media
9 Holdom Avenue, Bletchley, Milton Keynes, Bucks, MK1 1QR, UK
1820 Jet Stream Drive, Colorado Springs, CO 80921, USA
OM Authentic Media, Medchal Road, Jeedimetla Village,
Secunderabad 500 055, A.P., India
www.authenticmedia.co.uk
Authentic Media is a division of IBS-STL U.K., limited by
guarantee, with its Registered Office at Kingstown Broadway,
Carlisle, Cumbria CA3 0HA.   Registered in England & Wales No.
1216232. Registered charity 270162

British Library Cataloguing in Publication Data
A catalogue record for this book is available from the
British Library

ISBN-13: 978-1-86024-624-1

Cover Design by fourninezero design.
Print Management by Adare Carwin
Printed and bound in Great Britain by J.H. Haynes & Co.,
Sparkford

Contents

PART FOUR: Eternity and Antiquity

APPENDICES

Acknowledgements

Without the efforts of a variety of scholars this book would never have been written. I have freely plundered the brains of theologians and historians, reinterpreting their material for people like myself who do not have a natural intellectual grasp of some of the weightier aspects of our faith. In particular I am indebted to the following writers who mostly unknowingly (especially the deceased ones) helped me in my researches:

David Baron, David Bivin, Hershel Brand, Dan Cohn-Sherbok, David L. Cooper, Bob Doty, Rachmiel Frydland, Arnold Fruchtenbaum, Louis Ginzberg, Donald Hagner, Dan Juster, Arthur Kac, Joseph Klausner, Samuel Levine, Ron Moseley, Aaron Parry, Raphael Patai, David Pawson, Tony Pearce, H. Polano, Jacob Prasch, Jerry Rabow, Walter Riggans, Moshe Rosen, Risto Santala, Gershom Scholem, Roy A. Stewart, Geza Vermes, Marvin R. Wilson, Brad H. Young.

Then there were those who knowingly helped me. First, my son Simon, who identified early typos and inconsistencies, then my good friend Chris who carried on in this vein, but with the emphasis on narrative style and Bible content. I am so thankful to the three biblical scholars, David, Richard and Derek, who commented on the Jewish and Christian content and provided me with valuable insight and feedback. I am really blessed having access to such a mine of authority. Then there were those early readers – Julia, David, Kit, Lillian and Norma – who helped me to ensure that the whole thing was readable and educational. Finishing it all off, undying thanks to my censor, filter and quality control operative, also known as 'wifey', who found things that everyone else missed and ensured that it all made sense.

A cheesy but heartfelt prayer: I thank you, Lord, for giving me this opportunity to serve you with the gifts you have given me. Please use this little book to increase knowledge of you, faith in you and the progression of your Kingdom. May veils be lifted. Amen.

Preface

I will start at the end, the very last declaration in the Gospel account of Jesus.

> *'Jesus did many other things as well. If every one of them were written down, I suppose that even the whole world would not have room for the books that would be written' (Jn. 21:25).*

Well, it's just as well they weren't all written down, otherwise we'd all be drowning in a sea of books and the trees of this world would be just a memory.

We start with a rather large number: 181,026. It's the current number of books about Jesus available online through the Amazon bookshop. From *The Laughing Jesus* to *What Would Jesus Eat* and the *Jesus of Suburbia* we are presented with a puzzling plethora of academia, trivia and exotica. This man certainly made an impact, even on those who would claim otherwise, and what other figure from ancient history who wrote no book, never travelled far from his familiar haunts and died in his prime could compete with this impact on the human psyche and the publishing industry?

This book adds to that number, but if it does not lead the reader into a fuller understanding of the life and mission of the most remarkable man who has ever lived, I hang my head in shame. Because even if only one per cent of those 181,026 books are serious contributions, then a new book on Jesus still has to offer something special to warrant the months of blood, sweat and sleeplessness in the writing, to say nothing of freshness and relevance in the reading.

So, what's new? What is brought to the table here? As it's the third part of the '. . . *of many names'* trilogy, two clues to the structure and content of this book are evident to loyal readers. First, the story of Jesus will be threaded together through a dozen or so names associated with him, and secondly, there will be a Jewish angle.

This is not the first book that looks at Jesus through Jewish eyes. The Bible was there first, though many people have not yet woken up to that fact. As there are 4,962 other books available through Amazon with the words *Jewish Jesus* somewhere in the title, I am not treading on virgin territory. But there's no other book around that also includes the word *fresh* in the title, so there is my claim for uniqueness and I'm sticking to it!

If you declare a fresh approach to a subject, the claim really needs to be backed up. So again, the question is asked, what's new?

I will answer with a provocative statement, and that is, if anyone can stake a claim to knowing God better than most, it's the Jews. Paul said as much in Romans 9.4–5:

> *'Theirs is the adoption as sons; theirs the divine glory, the covenants, the receiving of the law, the temple worship and the promises. Theirs are the patriarchs, and from them is traced*

> *the human ancestry of Christ, who is God over all, for ever*
> *praised!'*

The Jews have been there, done that, bought the yarmulke. In any biography of God, the Jews take the role
of the first wife. Their sad story is told figuratively in the
book of Hosea. They marry young; it's a first love, raw
and exciting. But the young bride is restless, with a rov-
ing eye for a well-turned-out idol and, consequently, a
marriage breakdown and a separation sought. For the
ten tribes of Israel, a divorce is granted because of her
many adulteries (Jer. 3:7–9), but for the remnant, a relationship is maintained. The Lord eventually betroths
Himself to a new bride, a union not yet consummated,
but this new relationship is more inclusive, with
Gentiles grafted in to join the Jews of the remnant. So the
Jews were there at the beginning and have seen the good
times and the bad times, but have never ceased to search
for God, even while in exile, even under the severest
persecution.

Even when the world rejected them, the Jews never
stopped searching. Mostly, they haven't found what
they were looking for, but their search has uncovered
many jewels, if not always the pearl of great price. Those
jewels sparkle like stars in the sky, guiding those who
have a mind to follow to an understanding of the ways
of God that can be surprising and exhilarating. And it is
this search that forms the bedrock for this book.

When Nicodemus quizzed him about being born
again, Jesus gently mocked him, amazed that a Pharisee,
'Israel's teacher', failed to grasp his teaching. It was an
understandable reaction, because if anyone was qualified
to understand this new message it was he. Nicodemus
was in a privileged position, perhaps unequalled in history. Here was a learned man, thoroughly acquainted not

only with the Hebrew scriptures but with the whole body of Jewish thought, 'The Traditions of the Elders'. He spoke the language of Jesus and could read and write in Hebrew and Aramaic, the languages of the scriptures. And to cap it all, the greatest privilege of all, a one-to-one Bible study with the Son of God himself! We read of few such encounters, but there were undoubtedly more.

We are as far away from Nicodemus as it's possible to get. Not only are we denied the privilege of the personal encounter with Jesus in the flesh, but we also suffer in that we do not read and understand Holy Scripture in its original language, and although we may (or may not) be conversant with the scriptures, one glaring disadvantage of looking back two thousand years is that we are divorced from their culture, mindset, environment and religious heritage. A twenty-first-century sophisticate, living in a secular society and educated according to principles founded on the ideas of Greek philosophy, can have little natural empathy with a first-century religious culture founded on a Hebraic mindset.

Looking at the scriptures afresh with Jewish-tinted glasses can be a thrilling, invigorating, faith-expanding experience. This book offers you a tiny glimpse of the possibilities. Enjoy.

Introduction

We all have our own take on Jesus. Where do your ideas come from? They certainly didn't just pop into your mind out of nowhere. You put them there, consciously or otherwise. Now, thousands of books have been written about Jesus, and the views expressed didn't just pop into the authors' minds, they came from somewhere. Every author is writing from a given viewpoint. They may be Catholic, Pentecostal or Church of England, and will speak from within those traditions. They may be reformed, liberal or fundamentalist, and will argue from those positions. They may be speaking from such fringe areas as Mormonism or Jehovah's Witnesses and would want to incorporate their unique slant. Or they may be totally 'left field', insisting that Jesus was an astronaut/Venusian/peanut and *please buy my book so I can prove it to you.*

Discounting the lunatic fringe (you know who they are, even if they don't), the basic tools of the trade, apart from the scholarship and talent of the author, are the Bible as source material, the opinion of other commentators who agree with the position you are taking, and an assortment of other opinions which you are going to quote as a means of contrast. That's about it. Every serious book you have read about Jesus comes from the same structure – the Bible, your views and the views of others. And for a book to offer something new in the Jesus debate, it has to either come from a place that has rarely been mined before or extract its nuggets in new ways.

This book hopefully does both. It comes from a mindset lost to the ages. It comes from a culture that birthed and nurtured our Saviour. It comes from a religious system that ultimately denied him. And although much of the material has already been made available, a lot of it is from books of a bygone age, written in flowery language and arranged in labyrinthine paragraphs, or from the dusty halls of academia. Some remains in the hands of those who are simply not eager to share their findings, for religious reasons. This book has been written to share such knowledge in the true spirit of democracy, in such a way that even the author himself is able to understand it!

We will meet Jesus in surprising places. We will meet him at the very beginning of time, in the early days of the Jews and their struggles with God. We will see him as a fulfilment of unique promises, living as one among his people, teaching them how to live and how to understand him better. We will see what happened when his people failed to recognize him and how they covered up their mistake. We will then marvel at how some discovered him for themselves, despite incredible pressures both from within their own community and from the world that hated them in his name. Finally we will see him in power and splendour at the end of days.

This is a book mostly for followers of Jesus of Nazareth, but also for those who wonder what on earth it is all about. It's for those who are honest enough to admit that they don't have it 100 per cent, that they wouldn't last five minutes in a room with a highly motivated sceptic if they had to defend all aspects of his nature and ministry.

If you have given any thought to any of the following, then this book will help:

- How involved was Jesus in the creation of the universe?
- What did Jesus do before his incarnation?
- How can Jewish people not see Jesus as the fulfilment of Old Testament prophecies?
- How Jewish was Jesus?
- What exactly did Jesus do to make the religious leaders so angry?
- What was so special about Jesus' teaching methods?
- What title did Jesus most use for himself and why?
- What was the biggest mistake ever made and how was it covered up?
- How was the real Jesus hidden from ordinary Jews for nearly 1,500 years?
- How did some Jews find Jesus against all the odds?
- Who is going to be really surprised when Jesus returns?

Before we get started, there's one thing that needs to be made clear. Everything we need to know about Jesus with regard to our personal salvation is written in the Word of God, the Bible. This book is not going to uncover any lost truths that diminish or discredit this basic message in any way. The intention is to provide condiment for the feast, oil for the mental gears. Your faith will be gently bolstered, without leaving safe ground. Trust me: you will not be led astray.

The Bible is, as ever, our benchmark, anchor and foundation. Although we will be dipping into other Jewish writings on our journey, from the Aramaic Targums to the Hebrew and Aramaic Midrash and Talmud, these will be taken as illustration only, to confirm the Word of God, not to contradict it; to illuminate it, not to read doctrine into it.

Yet for most of you, this will mean venturing into unexplored territory. You will not be the first to dip your toe in the water of Jewish scholarship, but it can be a daunting experience for the untrained. So let me assure you that you will not be alone on this exhilarating voyage of discovery; you will receive all the gentle guidance you need. Although I have included a description and potted history of the Jewish literature we will be dipping into, in Appendix A at the end of this book, I will also set the scene for anything that may be unfamiliar to you as and when you need it.

This book will provide a dozen interlocking portraits of Jesus, each describing him from a different angle but all combining to provide a full picture. And the picture is so complete, so compelling, so awesome that you wonder why the Jews, particularly the learned religious scholars of the first century, missed the point!

The book is written for those Christians who are eager to go deeper into an understanding of Jesus Christ and are willing to explore the Jewish roots of their faith, without necessarily having any prior knowledge of such things. This is not another book for scholars, although there is much scholarship within its pages. My task has been to interpret the good work of biblical, religious and historical scholars into a meaningful narrative. To aid in this process, although all references from Scripture and religious documents are included, I have only rarely included direct quotes from academics, scholars and commentators. This is not petty arrogance, but is to ensure a consistent flow to the narrative. Nevertheless I have included details of books and articles referenced in notes at the end of each chapter, and have listed recommended books in Appendix B for your further study if you so wish.

Finally, remember what Paul said about the Jewish roots:

> '*Again I ask: Did they stumble so as to fall beyond recovery? Not at all! Rather, because of their transgression, salvation has come to the Gentiles to make Israel envious. But if their transgression means riches for the world, and their loss means riches for the Gentiles, <u>how much greater riches will their fulness bring</u>!*' *(Rom. 11:11–12)*

Greater riches for the world. This book is just a start!

Prologue

There is a form of Jewish Bible interpretation known as *Midrash*. It goes right back to Old Testament times and was well known by Jesus, who made use of it in his own teachings. It literally means to search or examine, and is the fruit of the questioning nature of the Jewish soul (both a blessing and a curse). For example, as a response to the commandment *'You shall not murder,'* Jews have urged God to be more specific. Is self-defence included here? What about suicide or warfare? This is Midrash. Inasmuch as the book of Deuteronomy repeats and comments on events and laws already given in the first four books of Moses, one could say that it is a Midrash on them.

Genesis Rabbah is a Midrash that comments on the book of Genesis. It was written around the fourth or fifth century AD, drawing on traditions passed down by word of mouth, and makes an interesting statement concerning things from before the dawn of time.

It tells us that six things were already in God's mind before the creation of the earth: the formation of Israel, the Throne of Glory, the Law (Torah), the building of the temple in Jerusalem, the coming of the Patriarchs, and the name of the Messiah.[1]

When I saw this list it tugged at my spirit, because there was a familiarity here that I couldn't put my finger on. Then it dawned on me and I looked up the passage in Paul's letter to the Romans where he was answering the rhetorical question, 'What have the Jews ever done for us?'

> *'Theirs is the adoption as sons; theirs the divine glory, the covenants, the receiving of the law, the temple worship and the promises. Theirs are the patriarchs, and from them is traced the human ancestry of Christ, who is God over all, for ever praised! Amen' (Rom. 9:4–5).*

Look again and compare these two lists. Virtually identical. I marvelled at this and thought through the implications. Here Paul did not just show his knowledge of the Jewish traditions, the 'Traditions of the Elders', but let the Holy Spirit guide him to use them in Scripture. And not just in any old place, but in this key passage that validates the Jewish people in the eyes of God. This suggests two things.

First, the content in these two passages suggests that what God had in mind before he 'lit the blue touch-paper' came to pass, and that the Jewish people were central to everything. No one could read these passages and doubt the importance of the Jews in God's eyes.

Secondly, although the Bible is our benchmark for discerning God's ways, we should not immediately discard all of these 'Traditions of the Elders'. The key is to let the Bible be the judge and have the final say on every matter. The fact is that on this matter the Bible has spoken, in Paul's letter to the Romans, and seems to suggest that there is an element of truth in the oral traditions concerning the events that preceded Creation.

This is key to the rest of this book, and at this point I want to make the following assertion:

The Bible is the literal and complete Word of God. All that is necessary for our salvation is in this book and there is nothing outside the Bible, in any Midrash or other 'Traditions of the Elders', that can gain you an iota of favour with God. Any biblical Christian would agree with this statement, I think.

For this book to be worth reading you would expect it to give insights into God's Word and into the life and mission of Jesus, and to provide these insights from Jewish traditions and observations. What you must realize, those of you who are just dipping your toes in the swirling currents of the Hebraic world, is that this is not a cunning attempt at 'Judaizing' you, distracting you from the straight path. Quite the reverse, really. The material in this book is going to enhance your spiritual journey, filling in the gaps that have always been there but have been largely unnoticed by a church that has lost its Jewish roots so long ago that it doesn't even realize that James and Jacob are the same name!

I will take this a little further and assure you that in this book, new insights brought from an examination of the Jewish literature will not only confirm existing biblical knowledge but will illuminate it and, as a result, boost your faith in a God who desires only that we should know Him better.

This is not a book to mock the church, to laugh at its mistakes and misconceptions. Believe me, when we examine how Jews have been treated historically at the hands of the church, there is little to laugh about. It's just about restoration, renewal and return.

> 'His purpose was to create in himself one new man out of the two [Jew and Gentile], thus making peace' (Eph. 2:15).

When Paul wrote these words in his letter to the Ephesians, he was an idealist: he saw the church of God as an equal partnership between Jew and Gentile. It never happened, but it's not too late now to start to restore what was lost.

Notes

[1] 'Six things preceded the creation of the world. Some of them were [actually] created, and some of them [merely] arose in the thought [of God] to be created. The Torah and the Throne of Glory were created. . . . The Fathers, Israel, the Temple and the name of the Messiah arose in the thought to be created . . .' (Genesis Rabbah 1:4)

PART ONE

The First Days

1

Memra

*Question: How involved was Jesus in the creation of
the universe?*

It all began one fine moment in eternity. All was God:
nothing else existed, because this was eternity, God's
special hangout, a place where He and only He lived
and still lives. Nothing else existed, because there would
be nowhere to put it and no time either, because neither
time nor place existed. All was God and all was fine.

It could have been like a whisper in the cool still
breeze or a shout, like the roar of Aslan. One thing it
wasn't was the Big Bang of the scientists, the random
inexplicable event. It was the voice of God and it kick-
started the universe. God spoke and time popped into
existence, and He called it the *Beginning*. Then God
breathed in and created some room and called it the
Heavens.

In the beginning God created the heavens and the earth.
These, the first words in the Christian and Jewish Bible,
are far more awesome than you could ever imagine and,
as we shall see, reveal an aspect of our Lord Jesus that is
truly mind-blowing.

Jesus? Now I was always led to believe that God the Father was the Creator of the universe and everything that we see around us. Doesn't the children's hymn tell us this?

> *All things bright and beautiful, all creatures great and small, all things wise and wonderful: the Lord God made them all.*

This is correct in a manner of speaking, until we examine the small print of Scripture. Our first port of call is the beginning of the Gospel of John, the New Testament equivalent of those mighty first words of Genesis:

> '*In the beginning was the Word, and the Word was with God, and the Word was God. He was with God in the beginning. Through him all things were made; without him nothing was made that has been made*' (*Jn. 1:1–3*).

Read these words, then repeat the first words of Genesis and let them sink into your spirit as I take you on a short journey.

At the time of Jesus, the common man living in the land tended not to speak Hebrew. The language of everyday conversation was Aramaic, a language imported by the conquering Assyrians and also brought back by Jews returning from Babylonian captivity centuries earlier. In synagogues, after readings were made from the Hebrew (Old Testament) scriptures, an official would recite an Aramaic paraphrase of those readings. These paraphrases were known as *Targums*. For a long time they had to be committed to memory, so that it could be clear that they didn't have the authority of written Hebrew Scripture. Eventually they were written down and a number of them became very popular, as they provided not only a translation of the scriptures but also a commentary on them by learned teachers of the day. When Jesus was dying on the cross and uttered the Aramaic phrase, '*Eloi, Eloi, lama sabachthani,*' scholars have suggested that he was quoting from the Targum on Psalm 22.

It starts to become interesting when we look at a Targum that was used to paraphrase the first chapter of Genesis. Let us look first at the creation of man in verse 27:

> '*So God created man in his own image, in the image of God he created him; male and female he created them.*'

In Targum Jonathan, we read the following rendition of verse 27:

> '*And the Memra of God created man in his likeness, in the likeness of God, God created, male and female created He them.*'

Spot the odd word out. It's not a misprint, it's an Aramaic word, *Memra*, and it means . . . 'word'. If I haven't confused you, at least I may have excited you as we begin to realize that this *Memra* represents a missing link between Jewish and Christian theology. This will hit home when we consider that *Memra*, when translated into Greek, becomes the word *logos*, which brings us back to John 1:1:

> '*In the beginning was the Word, and the Word was with God, and the Word was God.*'

Let's read it again, substituting the Greek word for 'Word', if you follow me:

> *'In the beginning was the Logos, and the Logos was with God, and the Logos was God.'*

And again, this time using the Aramaic word:

> *'In the beginning was the Memra, and the Memra was with God, and the Memra was God.'*

Where has that brought us? Well, as we know from this passage in John, the person being referred to as the *Word* is Jesus himself:

> *'The Word became flesh and made his dwelling among us'* (*Jn. 1:14*).

This becomes interesting when we return to our Targum paraphrase of Genesis 1:27 and replace the word *Memra* with Jesus:

> *'And (the) Jesus (of God) created man in his likeness, in the likeness of God, God created, male and female created He them.'*

Even more interestingly, this shows us that the concept of the Word of God as Creator was already familiar to Jewish minds when Jesus arrived on the scene. This hits home further when we also discover that the word *Memra* appears more than five hundred times in Targums, and that its usual meaning is to convey an aspect of God that relates to the physical world, particularly in situations where God appears or speaks to humankind. The *Memra* was seen as both an individual and yet a part of God, and was also the instrument of creation. Now who does that remind us of?

'In the beginning was the Word, and the Word was with God, and the Word was God. He was with God in the beginning. Through him all things were made; without him nothing was made that has been made.'

Jewish thinkers have always struggled with the idea of God, a spirit being, bringing forth matter, whether fiery suns or delicate flowers. The idea of God creating through a different aspect of Himself, an intermediate stage, had always been an acceptable concept. Even one of the most learned of Jewish sages, the Ramban, declared that an intermediate stage existed between spirit and matter, so we find that aspects of the Trinity are not so alien to the Jewish mind as modern rabbis might want you to believe. Jewish scholars have seen this all over the Creation account. When the Bible says, *'The Spirit of God was hovering over the waters'* (Gen. 1:2), they look at a parallel passage in Isaiah and see this as the 'spirit of the Messiah'.[1] When God said, *'Let there be light,'* they see the 'great light' of the Messiah.

The Messiah has made his appearance in our story. For Orthodox Jews, there is no more important subject, and although their understanding does not always tally with the Christian understanding of Messiah, this concept will be developed as we travel together on our voyage of discovery. But for now it is sufficient to accept that although He is One, God does not work alone. Remember, I ask you to accept this, not necessarily understand it, because, let's face it, if this were easily understood, there would be no need for evangelism, because the things of God would be laid out clearly for all to see. Faith is the missing link, the added ingredient in the mix. Without it, there would be no acceptance or understanding. Some things are meant to remain mysteries: we can skirt around the fringes with our imperfect fallen minds, but can never delve into the very heart of them until we stand in glory before the Lord.

So the Word of God, the *Memra*, is the means whereby God created the universe. This idea is reinforced in the Psalms:

> *'By the word of the* LORD *were the heavens made, their starry host by the breath of his mouth' (Ps. 33:6).*

When John introduced the idea of Jesus as the Word of God, this was not as alien to the Jews of his day as we are led to believe. Some have even suggested that John pinched his ideas from contemporary Greek philosophy, forgetting that he was just a poor Jewish fisherman and the only way he was able to write such monumental passages of Scripture as his Gospel, his letters and the Revelation of Jesus Christ was through the inspiration of the Holy Spirit. Unless, of course, you believe the Holy Spirit borrowed His ideas from the Greeks!

First-century Jews would read the opening chapter of John's Gospel and immediately recognize Jesus as the *Memra*. It would have caused them no problem at all. It troubled later generations of Jewish rabbis, though. (The reasons behind the Jewish rejection of Jesus are covered in my book *The People of Many Names*.) Because the concept of *Memra* so evidently pointed to Jesus and gave credence to the idea of the Trinity, we find that once the Targums had slipped from common usage, the subsequent holy writings of the rabbis, the Talmud, failed to mention the *Memra* in any significant way. It reminded them too much of the rejected Messiah, so it just dropped out of sight, a symptom of the hardening of heart that God inflicted on His people for His own reasons. This is highlighted by an entry in the *Jewish Encyclopedia*:

'In the ancient Church liturgy, adopted from the Synagogue, it is especially interesting to notice how often the term Logos, (this is the Greek word for the Memra) in the sense of "the Word by which God made the world, or made His Law or Himself known to man," was changed into "Christ." Possibly on account of the Christian dogma, rabbinic theology, outside of the Targum literature, made little use of the term "Memra."'[2]

So Jesus, the *Memra*, was the means by which the universe was created. He's not only our Saviour and Deliverer and future King, but he also put the whole thing together in the first place. In case you're still not sure about this, let's read from Paul's letter to the Colossians, speaking about Jesus:

'He is the image of the invisible God, the firstborn over all creation. For by him all things were created: things in heaven and on earth, visible and invisible, whether thrones or powers or rulers or authorities; all things were created by him and for him. He is before all things, and in him all things hold together' (Col. 1:15–17).

The first few words here confirm our developing theme of Jesus being the physical manifestation of God, the aspect of God concerned with the dirt and grime of the world. God is spirit and invisible, but Jesus is very visible, his image seen by many over a thirty-year life span in the first century. Yet as Graham Kendrick expresses in his song 'The Servant King', 'Hands that flung stars into space, to cruel nails surrendered.' We have been brought up with a particular image of Jesus, whether through paintings, icons or the medium of the cinema. Now try to imagine Robert Powell or Jim Caviezel alongside God at the Creation, flinging stars into space. It's just too much for our puny mortal brains to imagine. Didn't God say in the book of Job, '*Where were you when I laid the earth's foundation?*' (Job 38:4). There are some things that we just have to take God's word for. I'm happy with that; I'm quite willing to take it on trust that my Almighty Creator created the universe in the way He did, and if that was through the very same Jesus who died for me, a broken and bloodied first-century Jew, then it just makes me love Him even more and helps me to appreciate more fully the sacrifice He made for me.

The idea of the Word of God as Creator is more familiar to modern Jews than they would possibly admit. Their prayer book, the *Siddur*, includes the following prayer, recited before drinking water:

> '*Blessed are You,* LORD, *our God, King of the Universe, by whose word everything comes to be*' (emphasis mine).

But there's one group of people who have a lot of trouble with our view of Jesus, the *Memra* of God, the Creator of all.

There's a tapping on your front door. You open it to a couple of smiling, earnest and well-dressed Jehovah's Witnesses. They are sincere people, but on one very major point of theology they are sincerely wrong. This is how their Bible 'translates' John 1:1:

> '*In the beginning the Word was, and the Word was with God, and the Word was a god*' (Jn. 1:1, New World Translation).

Can you spot the difference? Of course you can. The JWs don't see Jesus as God, they see him as *a god*, a created being just like you and me, but a bit more important! If only these people had the understanding of the *Memra*, rather than the dodgy Bible translation of a nineteenth-

century Christian cult, surely the true light would dawn
on them. Next time they come visiting and you run out
of patience with them, hit them between the eyes with
the Jewish view of a Creator God, a view reinforced by
another scripture, in the letter to the Hebrews:

> 'In the past God spoke to our forefathers through the prophets
> at many times and in various ways, but in these last days he
> has spoken to us by his Son, whom he appointed heir of all
> things, and through whom he made the universe. The Son is the
> radiance of God's glory and the exact representation of his
> being, sustaining all things by his powerful word' (Heb. 1:1–3).

These verses just cement our understanding so far. Jesus,
the Son of God, was the means by which the universe
was created. He is also the image of God, expressed in
the grander manner of *the radiance of God's glory*. This is
also borne out by a commentary on the fourth verse in
Genesis 1 by the highly acclaimed eleventh-century
Jewish scholar Rashi. He identifies the Messiah as the
'great light', shining on all of creation, when God
declared that '*the light was good, and he separated the light
from the darkness*'.

And running through it all, the great unfathomable
mystery of Creation, whereby it all hangs together
through his powerful word, his *Memra*.

But once he had created the universe, he didn't just
sit back on his laurels, biding his time until the incarnation. The *Memra* of God still had plenty to do. Do you
remember what I said earlier – an aspect of God that
relates to the physical world, particularly in situations
where God appears or speaks to humankind? Since
Creation there have been plenty of occasions when God
has had to communicate with us: the Old Testament is
full of these episodes. We will read about some of them

in the next chapter, but let's have a look at a few now. We will read the Bible verses, followed by the Targum paraphrase.

> *'Then the* LORD *rained down burning sulphur on Sodom and Gomorrah – from the* LORD *out of the heavens' (Gen. 19:24).*

> *'And the Word [Memra] of the Lord caused to descend upon the peoples of Sodom and Gomorrah, brimstone and fire from the Lord in heaven' (Targum Jonathan).*

The Bible verse seems confusing, implying a transaction between God and Himself, but the Targum clarifies it by identifying the *Memra* as the agent of destruction.

> *'Abram believed the* LORD, *and he credited it to him as right-eousness' (Gen. 15:6).*

> *'And Abraham trusted in the Word [Memra] of the Lord, and He counted it to him for righteousness' (Targum Onkelos).*

This was Abram's great declaration of faith.

> *'So God said to Noah, "This is the sign of the covenant I have established between me and all life on the earth"' (Gen. 9:17).*

> *'And the Lord said to Noah, "this is the token of the covenant which I have established between My Word [Memra] and between all flesh that is upon the earth"' (Targum Onkelos).*

As you can see, according to the Targums, it is through the *Memra* that God makes covenants with His people. We can see another example of that:

> *'I will establish my covenant as an everlasting covenant between me and you and your descendants after you for the generations to come, to be your God and the God of your descendants after you' (Gen. 17:7).*

> *'And I will establish my covenant between My Word [Memra] and between you'* (Targum Onkelos*).*

And then, most exciting of all . . .

> *'But Israel will be saved by the LORD with an everlasting salvation; you will never be put to shame or disgraced, to ages everlasting' (Is. 45:17).*

> *'But Israel shall be saved by the Word [Memra] of the Lord with an everlasting salvation'* (Targum Jonathan).

The *Memra* is the means of salvation. But more of that later. Let's now return to the beginning of the beginning.

> *'In the beginning God created the heavens and the earth' (Gen. 1:1).*

Even though, as far as I'm aware, not all Targum material has survived to modern times, I'll take the massive liberty of suggesting the following Targum paraphrase for this verse:

> *'In the beginning the Word [Memra] of God created the heavens and the earth.'*

This is fully consistent with John 1:1 and the other New Testament scriptures already mentioned, placing Jesus as the agent of Creation. With that idea firmly in our minds we can delve further into the Genesis account and we notice that a lot of other things nicely fall into place.

We will start by examining the original Hebrew of this opening statement in the Bible.

'B'resheet barah Elohim et hashamayim ve'at ha'arets.'

Scholars have spent lifetimes examining just these seven words, but modern man (me included) is cursed with rather shorter attention spans, so I will simply tease out a couple of points, selected to shed further light on our understanding of the *Memra*.

First, the word *barah*, which is translated as *created*, is a singular word. This means that whoever is doing the creating is a single being. That is fine, until we look at what word is used for who is doing the creating. The word is *Elohim*, meaning God. But *Elohim* is a plural word, suggesting that more than one agency was involved here. This squares up with our understanding of *Memra* and, when we consider the next verse, '. . . *and the Spirit of God was hovering over the waters,'* we find the whole Trinity implied in the first two verses of the Bible.

'And God said, "Let there be light," and there was light.'

This is the very next verse in the Bible and, no, I'm not going to provide you with a verse by verse commentary on Genesis; it's just that all the juicy stuff is in these early verses. What I am drawing your attention to here is that God's act of creation all through the Genesis account is through His spoken Word, His *Memra*.

'And God said . . .'

This pattern is repeated through every day of Creation. The creation of the world was made through a series of ten pronouncements. God gave His Word in order to reveal Himself to humankind. It's a theme repeated right through the Bible. God uses His Word, first to create and then to reveal Himself to His Creation. This is the function of the *Memra* of God and this is Jesus in action way before his incarnation.

> *'Then God said, "Let us make man in our image, in our likeness, and let them rule over the fish of the sea and the birds of the air, over the livestock, over all the earth, and over all the creatures that move along the ground"' (Gen. 1:26).*

This verse has provoked much debate, to put it mildly, in both Jewish and Christian circles, as well as in areas where these circles overlap. The key point of interest is the fact that God talks in the plural: *'Let **us** make man in **our** image.'* Who on earth (and in the heavens) is He talking about? At one extreme, some early Jewish translators even deliberately mistranslated the words 'let us' as 'let me'.[3] Others have suggested that God was referring to a 'heavenly court' of angelic beings or that He was talking to Himself in a sense of chewing over an issue, or that He was using the royal 'we', as in Queen Victoria's 'We are not amused.' The Targum Neofiti, commenting on the next verse (verse 27), says:

> *'And the* Memra *of the Lord created the man in his (own) likeness.'*

Although there is also debate as to what exactly is meant by 'likeness' in the above two verses, it is consistent that Jesus, the God who became Man in His incarnation, would, at the moment of creation of the first man, have provided the template for the physical as well as the spiritual form of human beings.

In other words, the mystery is not that God took the form of man when Jesus was born to Mary in Bethlehem, but rather that Adam took the form of Jesus when God formed him from the dust of the ground. Just a thought. Interesting, eh?

One last word on the creation of Adam. Here is the second time it is mentioned in Genesis, in the next chapter:

> 'The LORD God formed the man from the dust of the ground and breathed into his nostrils the breath of life, and the man became a living being' (Gen. 2:7).

The Hebrew word used for 'formed' is unusual in that an extra letter is added to the word which is used later on in the chapter when it deals with the formation of the animals (verse 19). The letter is a yod; in the 'formation of man' verse it appears twice, but in the 'formation of animals' verse it appears only once. In the Midrash on Genesis, this is explained by the fact that Adam was created with a dual nature, a soul as well as a body, whereas animals have a single nature: a body but no soul.

So, you would agree that knowledge of ancient Jewish writings can enhance our understanding of the scriptures. It's one thing blindly accepting the fact that Jesus, the second member of the Trinity, was somehow involved in Creation, but another thing to marvel at how the Aramaic Targums, written in biblical times, can fill in the gaps. Added credibility is given when you realize that the last thing that Jewish scholars would want to provide is a Christian apologetic, yet that is what they have done. The fact is that the role of the *Memra* seems to square up more with Christian theology than with the rigid structures of Judaism. There is a ring of truth about all this that warms the soul and encourages us to want to find out more. So let us do so.

Before we move on, a quick word of explanation for the pedantic ones among you. When I posed the question 'How involved was Jesus in the creation of the universe?' at the head of this chapter, there was a semantic oddity implied. In plain English, something didn't quite scan. 'Jesus' is our familiar name for the Son of God, though it wasn't a flesh-and-blood 'Jesus' who was present at the creation of the universe, it was the *Memra*. So when I refer to the Man of Many Names throughout this book as Jesus, I am merely using, for convenience, the name that we know best for the Son of God. I hope that is now clear and I will move on.

Our story continues as we begin our journey through the Hebrew scriptures.

Notes

1   Midrash Rabbah on Isaiah 11:2.
2   *The Jewish Encyclopedia* (New York and London, 1904), p. 465.
3   As stated in D.J.A. Clines, 'The Image of God in Man', *Tyndale Bulletin* (1968), p. 62, referring to J. Jervell, *Imago Dei* (Gottingen, 1960), p. 75, and taken from http://www.jewsforjesus.org/publications/issues/10_8/trinity.

2

The Angel of the LORD

Question: What did Jesus do before his incarnation?

There had been times in the early history of God's people when He simply needed to have a stiff word with them. At those times, sending them a dream or vision or a rank-and-file angel was not enough; He really needed to confront them – personally. There was only one snag, as God once said to Moses:

> *'You cannot see my face, for no-one may see me and live' (Ex. 33:20).*

So what could He do? On these occasions He sent the Angel of the LORD. Let's read about the first such biblical encounter.

> *'The angel of the LORD found Hagar near a spring in the desert; it was the spring that is beside the road to Shur. And he said, "Hagar, servant of Sarai, where have you come from, and where are you going?" "I'm running away from my mistress Sarai," she answered. Then the angel of the LORD told her, "Go back to your mistress and submit to her." The angel added, "I*

*will so increase your descendants that they will be too numer-
ous to count." The angel of the* LORD *also said to her: "You are
now with child and you will have a son. You shall name him
Ishmael, for the* LORD *has heard of your misery"' (Gen.
16:7–11).*

Isn't that interesting that the Angel of the LORD would
make his first cameo appearance not to Abraham, the
first patriarch of the Jews and hero of the faith, but to a
pagan slave girl whose descendants would give rise to
the Arab people? God just doesn't follow the rules, does
He? He finds her in a state of despair, having run away
from Abram's camp, and He speaks with the greatest
authority to assure her of her own future and that of her
descendants. Later, when she leaves camp for the final
time with her son, Ishmael, the Angel of the LORD again
communicates with her and repeats the promises.

*'"What is the matter, Hagar? Do not be afraid; God has heard
the boy crying as he lies there. Lift the boy up and take him by
the hand, for I will make him into a great nation"' (Gen.
21:17–18).*

So God was so keen to give assurances as to the future
of the Arab peoples that He sent His special envoy. You
would expect Him to do the same for the Jewish people
and He does, at the one key moment when the fate of the
entire Jewish race hung by a thread, or rather by a sharp
blade. Abraham stood over his beloved son, Isaac, ready
to slit his throat . . .

'But the angel of the LORD *called out to him from heaven,
"Abraham! Abraham!" "Here I am," he replied. "Do not lay a
hand on the boy," he said. "Do not do anything to him. Now I
know that you fear God, because you have not withheld from*

me your son, your only son." Abraham looked up and there in
a thicket he saw a ram caught by its horns. He went over and
took the ram and sacrificed it as a burnt offering instead of his
son. So Abraham called that place The LORD Will Provide.
And to this day it is said, "On the mountain of the LORD it
will be provided." The angel of the LORD called to Abraham
from heaven a second time and said, "I swear by myself,
declares the LORD, that because you have done this and have
not withheld your son, your only son, I will surely bless you
and make your descendants as numerous as the stars in the sky
and as the sand on the seashore"' (Gen. 22:11–17).

Again, the Angel of the LORD had sufficient authority to
make promises concerning Abraham and his descendants, the people of Israel.

This was the *Akeidah*, the Binding of Isaac, the most
read, recited and prayed-over story in Judaism. There are
also striking parallels here with the birth of Jesus. Both are
promised sons, born as a result of a miraculous concep-
tion (or at least highly improbable in the case of Isaac, on
account of the age of his parents!). Both are offered up as
a sacrifice, and although Jesus succumbs to death on the
cross, in the longer term both live on. Interestingly they
were also both of similar age. Although Christian tradition places Isaac in late childhood, the Hebrew word used
for him, *naar*, best describes him as a bachelor of mar-
riageable age. In fact Jewish tradition places Isaac at
around 36 years old, on account of his mother's death
soon after this episode at the age of 127, which was 37
years after his (improbable) birth when she was at the ripe
old age of 90. If we accept this scenario, we concede that
Abraham was 100 years old at the Binding of Isaac and in
no position to forcefully control the situation. Therefore
Isaac must have been a willing sacrifice, rather than a
helpless youth. An interesting thought.

The location of this famous episode was Moriah, the very place, as the Midrash tells us, where Adam made the first altar, demolished by the Flood and then rebuilt by Noah. It was said to be directly under God's throne of glory in heaven and the exact location of the future temple to be built in the great city of Jerusalem. The very name of Jerusalem, *Yerushalayim* in Hebrew, was said to be the result of a compromise by God. We are told that Abraham wanted to call the place *Adonai Yireh*, meaning 'God will look down on this place and shower the world with goodness', but the oldest living patriarch, Shem, the son of Noah (how old must he have been?) wanted to name it *Shalaim*, the 'city of perfection'. God added these two names together to make *Yerushalayim*, meaning that the holiness of the city would be such that God would want to bless the whole world. If this is so, it is something that the world can truly look forward to, and which is confirmed by the Word of God when it predicts events that may perhaps be nearer than we imagine:

> '*Then the survivors from all the nations that have attacked Jerusalem will go up year after year to worship the King, the* LORD *Almighty, and to celebrate the Feast of Tabernacles . . . On that day* HOLY TO THE LORD *will be inscribed on the bells of the horses, and the cooking pots in the* LORD'S *house will be like the sacred bowls in front of the altar. Every pot in Jerusalem and Judah will be holy to the* LORD *Almighty, and all who come to sacrifice will take some of the pots and cook in them*' (Zech. 14:16,20–21).

Now we skip a generation after Abraham to find that the next encounter is in a dream with Jacob.

> '*The angel of God said to me in the dream, "Jacob." I answered, "Here I am." And he said, "Look up and see that all*

the male goats mating with the flock are streaked, speckled or spotted, for I have seen all that Laban has been doing to you. I am the God of Bethel, where you anointed a pillar and where you made a vow to me. Now leave this land at once and go back to your native land"' (Gen. 31:11–13).

Has the Angel of the LORD exceeded his station here? He is not just giving Jacob direct and far-reaching instructions but he is claiming to be God. Has pride taken over? No, it's not an angel making a bid for the top job. That's already happened once before and the whole of humankind is still paying for it!

When the Angel of the LORD announces that he is the God of Bethel (literally, the God of the 'house of God'), he is telling the truth. There can be no other sensible conclusion than that the Angel of the LORD is God Himself. These appearances are known as *theophanies*, from the Greek, meaning 'seeing or showing God'. When the Bible speaks of the Angel of the LORD making an appearance, you can be assured that it's God Himself showing up.

But didn't we read that '*You cannot see my face, for no-one may see me and live*' (Ex. 33:20)? True, if Father God makes an appearance.

This is why the Angel of the LORD seems to be none other than Jesus himself, the *Memra* of God, making pre-incarnation appearances. After all, as Jesus himself tells us in John 14:9, '*Anyone who has seen me has seen the Father,*' and this is why these encounters were not fatal, as threatened. Yet one nearly was:

'*Now Moses was tending the flock of Jethro his father-in-law, the priest of Midian, and he led the flock to the far side of the desert and came to Horeb, the mountain of God. There the angel of the LORD appeared to him in flames of fire from within a bush. Moses saw that though the bush was on fire it did not burn up. So Moses thought, "I will go over and see this strange sight – why the bush does not burn up." When the* LORD *saw that he had gone over to look, God called to him from within the bush, "Moses! Moses!" And Moses said, "Here I am." "Do not come any closer," God said. "Take off your sandals, for the place where you are standing is holy ground." Then he said, "I am the God of your father, the God of Abraham, the God of Isaac and the God of Jacob." At this, Moses hid his face, because he was afraid to look at God' (Ex. 3:1–6).*

This ought to be the clincher to our argument. The Angel of the LORD here uses the ineffable Name of God, the closest we get to His personal name. The place is also designated as holy ground. No ordinary angel would utter this name and expect no consequence. No ordinary angel would have the cheek to declare the place of his visitation as holy ground. As with the Isaac episode, this is a key moment in the life of God's people and there's no wonder that God makes an appearance, in the form of the Angel of the LORD.

There is added significance in the Midrash, which examines the bush itself. It asks, 'Why a burning bush?' and suggests that just as the bush burns but is not destroyed, so the children of Israel (and the Jews throughout history) suffer but are never destroyed. Here the Midrash is giving added colour to the biblical account. It is not replacing it or contradicting it, but drawing out meanings that aid our understanding of God's Word.

Later in the career of Moses, when he leads the children of Israel out of Egypt, we see that they had their own GPS (God's Positioning System) to help them.

> '*By day the* LORD *went ahead of them in a pillar of cloud to guide them on their way and by night in a pillar of fire to give them light, so that they could travel by day or night. Neither the pillar of cloud by day nor the pillar of fire by night left its place in front of the people*' (Ex. 13:21–22).

Wait a minute, isn't this God Himself?

> '*Then the angel of God, who had been travelling in front of Israel's army, withdrew and went behind them. The pillar of cloud also moved from in front and stood behind them*' (Ex. 14:19).

No, it's the Angel of the LORD, this time identified with pillars of cloud and fire.

Moses speaks more of this Angel of the LORD. This individual would have the authority of God Himself.

> '*See, I am sending an angel ahead of you to guard you along the way and to bring you to the place I have prepared. Pay attention to him and listen to what he says. Do not rebel against him; he will not forgive your rebellion, since my Name is in him. If you listen carefully to what he says and do all that I say, I will be an enemy to your enemies and will oppose those who oppose you. My angel will go ahead of you and bring you into the land of the Amorites, Hittites, Perizzites, Canaanites, Hivites and Jebusites, and I will wipe them out*' (Ex. 23:20–23).

Rashi, the most influential Jewish commentator of the Middle Ages, suggested that the words '*since my name is in him*' mean, '*He and I have the same name.*' More of this later.

The Angel of the LORD also features in the story of Balaam and his commission to curse the Jews. We find

God taking a very serious interest in this episode (Num. 22 – 23), and it's the Angel of the LORD who is dispatched to thwart Balaam and speak to him through the mouth of his ass.

Other appearances of the Angel of the LORD are in the time of the Judges, when he reminds the people of their disobedience and their breaking of the Covenant (Judg. 2:1–5), has a cosy chat with Gideon under the oak tree to empower him for service (Judg. 6:11–24), and tells the parents of Samson about the great son they are going to bring into the world. This is an interesting story because through it we find out a bit more about the Angel of the LORD. We find out that he has the appearance of both man and angel (Judg. 13:6), but we get a clear declaration of his identity when Manoah, Samson's father, asks for his name. He doesn't give it, but once a burnt offering has been made the following happens:

> *'As the flame blazed up from the altar towards heaven, the angel of the* LORD *ascended in the flame. Seeing this, Manoah and his wife fell with their faces to the ground. When the angel of the* LORD *did not show himself again to Manoah and his wife, Manoah realised that it was the angel of the* LORD. *"We are doomed to die!" he said to his wife. "We have seen God!"'* (Judg. 13:20–22)

So Manoah knew exactly who he was dealing with: God Himself. And because he didn't exactly die as a result, it was God in the form of Jesus, the *Memra* of God.

It was the Angel of the LORD who ministered to Elijah when he was on the run from Jezebel after the showdown on Mount Carmel (1 Kgs. 19) and who prompted King David to build an altar on the site where the great temple would be built (1 Chron. 21:18). The fiercer side of his nature was shown when he put to death 185,000

Assyrian soldiers who were surrounding Jerusalem (2 Kgs. 19:35).

In fact it's amazing how many familiar Old Testament stories include dealings with the *Memra* of God, through the Angel of the LORD.

It is time to venture a little deeper, to further cement this idea of Jesus' appearances to his people, in the guise of the Angel of the LORD. One passage of Scripture that really sets the seal on this comes from the book of Isaiah:

> *'I will tell of the kindnesses of the* LORD, *the deeds for which he is to be praised, according to all the* LORD *has done for us – yes, the many good things he has done for the house of Israel, according to his compassion and many kindnesses. He said, "Surely they are my people, sons who will not be false to me"; and so he became their Saviour. In all their distress he too was distressed, and the angel of his presence saved them. In his love and mercy he redeemed them; he lifted them up and carried them all the days of old' (Is. 63:7–9).*

Here God states that He is to be the Saviour of His people, but that it was actually the Angel of His presence (of the LORD) that did the saving. The only Saviour we know, of course, is Jesus Christ, so what we present here is a pretty strong case that the Angel of the LORD is Jesus Himself. Perhaps the clincher is the fact that the Angel of the LORD appears nowhere in the Gospels, because even Jesus couldn't appear in two places at the same time!

Finally, there is that curious incident in Jacob's life:

> *'So Jacob was left alone, and a man wrestled with him till daybreak. When the man saw that he could not overpower him, he touched the socket of Jacob's hip so that his hip was wrenched as he wrestled with the man. Then the man said, "Let me go, for it is daybreak." But Jacob replied, "I will not let you go*

> unless you bless me." The man asked him, "What is your
> name?" "Jacob," he answered. Then the man said, "Your name
> will no longer be Jacob, but Israel, because you have struggled
> with God and with men and have overcome." Jacob said,
> "Please tell me your name." But he replied, "Why do you ask
> my name?" Then he blessed him there. So Jacob called the
> place Peniel, saying, "It is because I saw God face to face, and
> yet my life was spared"' (Gen. 32:24–30).

It starts off as a scuffle, though a rather prolonged one, with
the deadlock broken only by an illegal move. By the end of
the story we realize that Jacob has had an encounter with
God, an encounter so profoundly significant that Jacob is
renamed. His protagonist is both man and God, so could it
be Jesus himself who fought that extended bout?

The final word takes us back to the burning bush.
Compare God's words when Moses asked Him to identify Himself, with Jesus' words to the Pharisees when
they asked him to do the same.

> 'God said to Moses, "I AM WHO I AM. This is what you are to
> say to the Israelites: 'I AM has sent me to you'"' (Ex. 3:14)."

> '"I tell you the truth," Jesus answered, 'before Abraham was
> born, I am!"' (Jn. 8:58)

The words should speak loud and clear to you and will
be further analysed in Chapter 7.

So we rest our case. Jesus was far from idle between
Creation and Incarnation. God did not just light the blue
touchpaper and let His angels get on with the process of
guiding His covenant people through the trials and
struggles of establishing themselves and fulfilling the
role assigned to them. Not only was He totally in charge
at all times, but at certain turning points, such as the

Binding of Isaac and the burning bush, He had to make a personal appearance. These were the appearances of the Angel of the LORD, none other than Jesus himself, and we can only marvel that we have a God unafraid to get His hands dirty for no other reason than the fact that He loves us so much.

3

The Promised One

Question: How can Jewish people not see Jesus as the
fulfilment of Old Testament prophecies?

This is going to be a long chapter. But it is an important
one because we are going to meet someone new within
the pages of the Old Testament. As he isn't always
named, I am going to call him *the Promised One*. Some
call him the Messiah, but he is usually not specifically
identified as such, although it's really just a matter of
semantics. At Christmas time we meet him through song
and sermon but we rarely get a full picture. I am going
to attempt to provide that full picture, which is why this
chapter is so long. My approach is to concentrate on the
key battlegrounds, verses that Jewish scholars accuse
Christians of hijacking, reading into them signposts to
Jesus. By concentrating on the Jewish objections and
dealing with them we will build up the fullest picture of
this Promised One, which will enable us to see how close
a fit Jesus really is. After all, the scriptures were originally given to the Jewish people, in their language and
using familiar patterns of thought and literary styles.
One would expect Jewish objections to be considered

and authoritative, so we can expect to learn much through engaging with their concerns.

But before we embark on our journey it must be stated that there seem to be two Promised Ones spoken of within the pages of the Old Testament. This has been an area of controversy because Jewish scholars have quite rightly explained that in no way could Jesus, in his first-century ministry, have fulfilled both of them. In this they are correct, and this will be explored in a later chapter. But first things first: we must learn to be patient. To use an example from the kitchen, we are first going to use a sieve with large holes to separate out the larger lumps, before we make use of the one with smaller holes to pick out the rest.

You probably know the story. A few hours after Jesus' resurrection, Cleopas and his companion are strolling over to Emmaus, chatting about the awesome events of the day. Jesus appears and joins in their discussion. They are kept from recognizing him and it is clear from their words that they fail to understand the reasons behind Jesus' mission. Finally Jesus turns to them . . .

> *'And beginning with Moses and all the Prophets, he explained to them what was said in all the Scriptures concerning himself' (Lk. 24:27).*

So the scriptures spoke of him. These were, obviously, what we call the Old Testament, the only holy writ available to the Jews of Jesus' day. These were the Hebrew scriptures, known to Jews ancient and modern as the *Tanakh*.

The *Complete Jewish Bible*, a modern translation by David Stern, a Jewish Christian, acknowledges this in his take on the above verse:

> *'Then, starting with Moshe and all of the prophets, he explained to them the things that can be found throughout the Tanakh concerning himself.'*

This word is a Hebrew acronym, **Tanakh**, comprising the three parts of the Hebrew scriptures: the *Torah*, the *Nevi'im* and the *Ketuvim*.

The Tanakh is made up of exactly the same books as the Old Testament, but arranged differently, in the order that we consider them below.

Torah, often mistranslated as 'Law', is more correctly translated as 'Teachings' or 'Instruction'. It is made up of the first five books of the Hebrew scriptures: Genesis, Exodus, Leviticus, Numbers and Deuteronomy, the five books of Moses.

Nevi'im are the prophetic books, though not necessarily the ones you would expect. Let's have a roll-call.

Usual suspects: the major prophets – Isaiah, Jeremiah, Ezekiel; the minor prophets, also called 'the Twelve' – Hosea, Joel, Amos, Obadiah, Jonah, Micah, Nahum, Habakkuk, Zephaniah, Haggai, Zechariah, Malachi.

Surprise entrants: these are the books that Christians know as the histories – Joshua, Judges, 1 Samuel, 2 Samuel, 1 Kings and 2 Kings.

Startling omission: Daniel – surely not?

Ketuvim are the 'Writings', consisting of the Psalms, Proverbs, Job, Song of Songs, Ruth, Lamentations, Ecclesiastes, Esther, Daniel, Ezra, Nehemiah, and ending with 1 and 2 Chronicles, the final books in the Hebrew scriptures.

So why is the book of Daniel, considered one of the prophetic books in the Christian Bible, not classified as a prophetic book in the Jewish Bible? Why is it not in the Nevi'im, along with Isaiah, Jeremiah and Hosea?

Was Daniel not a prophet? How strange. This is worth examining.

The Talmud, the great body of Jewish thought compiled from the second century AD, declares that there were thousands of Hebrew prophets in biblical times, in fact twice as many as left Egypt in the Exodus, but only those with a message for future generations were considered important enough to make the master list.[1] This list comprised forty-eight male prophets, from Abraham to Malachi, and seven female prophets, from Sarah to Esther. Apparently Daniel was on the original list, but the scholar Rashi did not consider him a prophet and had him replaced.[2]

Rashi is probably the best known commentator on the Hebrew scriptures, so if he had a serious objection to Daniel's inclusion in the master list it must have been a good one. His stated reason was that to be qualified as a prophet one had to cater to the needs of people living in one's own time. As Daniel's prophecies were for the future, in Rashi's view this disqualified him. In his commentary on the Talmud, Rashi accepts that Daniel was a prophet, but not one sent with a prophetic message for his people in his own day.[3]

Yet even to this untrained mind, something is not right here. Daniel was very much a man of his day, and although interpretations of his words were for the future, he also spoke to the people of his day. And despite the fact that his prophecies were not for the present, *prophecies* they still were. No less an authority than Jesus himself confirms the standing of Daniel. In Matthew 24:15 he calls him '*the prophet Daniel*'. But of course, Rashi and the rabbis don't share our confidence in Jesus as the final word.

Rashi lived at a time when state 'Christianity' was at its most rampant and violent, particularly in its attitude towards the Jews. His latter years were saddened by the massacres which took place during the first Crusade, in which he lost relatives and friends, many killed after refusing to convert to Christianity. He had every reason to be most unsympathetic to the Christian religion and would consider the denial of Daniel as a prophet a key victory, particularly as Daniel is considered by Christian scholars as the *key* to New Testament prophecy.

Why would this be? The fact is that within the book of Daniel there are a number of prophecies that can be said to be fulfilled by Jesus Christ or his church. If indeed this was so, Rashi and other Jewish commentators would have been very aware of it, even if a few prophecies could be considered ambiguous or contentious. The last thing they would want would be for Jews to read the book of Daniel as a prophetic book and come to some uncomfortable conclusions.

Perhaps the most telling prophecy was that in Daniel 9:20–27. First the preamble:

> 'While I was speaking and praying, confessing my sin and the sin of my people Israel and making my request to the LORD my God for his holy hill – while I was still in prayer, Gabriel, the man I had seen in the earlier vision, came to me in swift flight about the time of the evening sacrifice. He instructed me and said to me, "Daniel, I have now come to give you insight and understanding. As soon as you began to pray, an answer was given, which I have come to tell you, for you are highly esteemed. Therefore, consider the message and understand the vision: 'Seventy "sevens" are decreed for your people and your holy city to finish transgression, to put an end to sin, to atone for wickedness, to bring in everlasting righteousness, to seal up vision and prophecy and to anoint the most holy.'"'

Then the bombshell:

> *'Know and understand this: From the issuing of the decree to restore and rebuild Jerusalem until the Anointed One, the ruler, comes, there will be seven "sevens", and sixty-two "sevens". It will be rebuilt with streets and a trench, but in times of trouble. After the sixty-two "sevens", the Anointed One will be cut off and will have nothing. The people of the ruler who will come will destroy the city and the sanctuary.'*

What this couple of verses gives us is first a timetable for the appearance of the Anointed One, then a glimpse into what will be in store for him, and finally a prediction of the destruction of Jerusalem and the holy temple after his demise (his 'cutting off').

The Anointed One will appear after a period of seven 'sevens' and sixty-two 'sevens' following the order to restore and rebuild Jerusalem. There's more unpacking to be done here than in a royal house swap!

The Anointed One, the ruler, is none other than the promised Messiah. This is easy, as both expressions mean the same thing. The English word 'Messiah' is simply a transliteration of the Hebrew *Mashiach*, meaning 'the Anointed One'.

Now, as for these numbers, it's all a bit convoluted, isn't it?

First, we need to understand what is meant by 'sevens'. In the English translation of the Hebrew text (known as the Masoretic text), the word used is actually translated as 'week'. So we have seven weeks, then sixty-two weeks. These are not actual weeks of seven days: what we have here is known as a *shemittah cycle*, a seven-year period that parallels a seven-day week, particularly the seven days of Creation. There is nothing controversial about this usage; it is a standard Jewish understanding: so 'sevens' means 'seven years'. For the last word on this, read Leviticus 25:8, where it talks of 'seven Sabbaths of years' as a period of forty-nine years, the Sabbath being the seventh day of the week.

With that understanding we can return to the verses . . .

> *'From the issuing of the decree to restore and rebuild Jerusalem*
> *until the Anointed One, the ruler, comes, there will be 49 years*
> *and 434 years [i.e. 483 years] . . . After the 434 years, the*
> *Anointed One will be cut off and will have nothing.'*

So, if we know the starting point and then add 483 years, we should reach the point where the Messiah *'will be cut off and will have nothing'*.

Interestingly, we do know the starting point: in fact it is a historical certainty. The *'issuing of the decree to restore and rebuild Jerusalem'* was fulfilled in the actions of Artaxerxes I, who in 444 BC made an order that the walls of Jerusalem should be rebuilt.

> *'In the month of Nisan in the twentieth year of King*
> *Artaxerxes, when wine was brought for him, I took the wine and*
> *gave it to the king. I had not been sad in his presence before; so*
> *the king asked me, "Why does your face look so sad when you*
> *are not ill? This can be nothing but sadness of heart." I was very*
> *much afraid, but I said to the king, "May the king live for ever!*
> *Why should my face not look sad when the city where my*
> *fathers are buried lies in ruins, and its gates have been destroyed*
> *by fire?" The king said to me, "What is it you want?" Then I*
> *prayed to the God of heaven, and I answered the king, "If it*
> *pleases the king and if your servant has found favour in his*
> *sight, let him send me to the city in Judah where my fathers are*
> *buried so that I can rebuild it." Then the king, with the queen*
> *sitting beside him, asked me, "How long will your journey take,*
> *and when will you get back?" It pleased the king to send me; so*
> *I set a time. I also said to him, "If it pleases the king, may I have*
> *letters to the governors of Trans-Euphrates, so that they will*

> *provide me safe-conduct until I arrive in Judah? And may I*
> *have a letter to Asaph, keeper of the king's forest, so he will give*
> *me timber to make beams for the gates of the citadel by the tem-*
> *ple and for the city wall and for the residence I will occupy?"*
> *And because the gracious hand of my God was upon me, the*
> *king granted my requests' (Neh. 2:1–8).*

The first part of the Daniel prophecy mentioned forty-nine years, which most commentators suggest is the time that it took to finish the rebuilding job. This may seem a long time, but then again how long was it meant to take to rebuild a certain football stadium in modern London, with all the sophistication of modern building science available?

Now the maths gets a little complex, when we add up the years from 444 BC to get to the time of the Messiah.[4] It's not straightforward, for the simple reason that biblical events didn't happen in modern Europe! We measure our years by the time it takes the earth to travel completely round the sun. This is called a *solar year* and it takes just over 365 days. The Jewish calendar is different: it is based on the moon and the time it takes to revolve round the earth. This is a lunar calendar, where a year consists of only 360 days. So when the Bible speaks of years, these are '360-day' years, not '365-and-a-bit-day' years. So . . . pause for breath . . . adding 483 Jewish years to 444 BC, then converting back to our solar year, we arrive at around the year AD 33.

So, returning to our verses . . .

> *'At around AD 33, the Anointed One will be cut off and will*
> *have nothing.'*

This is incredible, when we consider how many Messiahs appeared at around that time only to be killed (cut off) in AD 33. Only one fits that profile: Jesus of Nazareth. It's an awesome prophecy. No wonder Rashi was adamant that Daniel wasn't a prophet!

Nevertheless, whether or not Rashi and the rabbis considered Daniel to be a prophetic book, if a scripture in the Hebrew Bible seems to point to a Messiah dying in AD 33, then we must believe that the rabbis have a response to this.

They scream '*mistranslation!*' Their response is a hard one to contest, as the scriptures are the Hebrew scriptures, written in *their* language, Hebrew.

To remind you, here is how we read the verse:

> '*Know and understand this: From the issuing of the decree to restore and rebuild Jerusalem until the Anointed One, the ruler, comes, there will be seven "sevens", and sixty-two "sevens". It will be rebuilt with streets and a trench, but in times of trouble.*'

Here is what the Masoretic Text, the translation used by Jewish readers, says for that verse:

> '*Know therefore and understand, that from the going forth of the commandment to restore and to build Jerusalem unto an anointed prince, shall be seven weeks: and threescore and two weeks shall the street be built again, and the wall, even in troublous times.*'

There are two key differences.

Where the Christian translation talks of *the* Anointed One, the Jewish translation speaks of *an* anointed prince. In short, the Christian interpretation speaks of a single individual, whereas the other one leaves the field open to anyone who is anointed, a list that could include kings, princes and assorted dignitaries.

Secondly, and significantly, there is a punctuation issue, a matter of a single colon. The Jewish translation splits up the seven weeks and the sixty-two weeks, declaring that the anointed prince came after seven weeks (forty-nine years), identified as King Cyrus of Persia, and that the sixty-two weeks (434 years) are the time until yet another rebuilding of Jerusalem.

This is key, and you begin to wonder how a string of Hebrew words in the original manuscripts of the Hebrew scriptures can be interpreted in two different ways. Does the Hebrew refer to *the* Anointed or *an* anointed? Does it speak of a period of forty-nine years or 434 years to his appearance? The task is made harder when you realize that these Hebrew scriptures were written without vowels or punctuation, and as divinely authored as these words are, it has always been down to Jewish and Christian scholars to discern their exact meaning. We can be assured that the original Hebrew scriptures are 100 per cent the Word of God, but we can never have this total assurance with those who tease the meaning of the words into English. Otherwise why are there over twenty major translations of the Bible into English – NIV, KJV, RSV, CEB and others – with more no doubt still on their way?

It's all a matter of interpretation, pertinently so for those contentious passages. Like Daniel 9:25, for instance. It is interesting to see that every major Christian Bible translation takes the party line on this passage except one. The Revised Standard Version (RSV) agrees with the Jewish interpretation and therefore does not speak of the Anointed One appearing on the scene and dying in AD 33. But then, this is what a scholar, R. Laird Harris, said about the RSV Bible translation:

> '*It is a curious study to check the Revised Standard Version of the Bible, a monument of higher critical scholarship, and note*

*how every important Old Testament passage purporting to
predict directly the coming of Christ has been altered so as to
remove this possibility . . . It is almost impossible to escape the
conclusion that the admittedly higher critical bias of the translators has operated in all of these places. The translations given
are by no means necessary from the Hebrew and in some cases
. . . are in clear violation of the Hebrew.'[5]*

So where is all this leading us? We are faced with a verse,
Daniel 9:25, that is one of the key verses used by
Christians to point to Jesus. Yet Jewish scholars and the
compilers of the RSV Bible read the verse in a totally different way. They add a colon halfway through the verse
and the whole meaning changes. The question we must
ask is: how did that colon get there in the first place if the
original Hebrew text had no punctuation?

The answer is simple. I have already mentioned that
the Jews use what is called the *Masoretic* text of the
Hebrew scriptures. The Masoretes were the Jewish
scholars in the ninth and tenth centuries AD who added
the vowels and punctuation for the worldwide Jewish
community. It was they who added the colon, called an
atnach, halfway through Daniel 9:25 and, by doing so,
sheared away the Messianic branch of expectation. With
a tiny flourish of the quill they invalidated any claim
that Jesus might have had to be the prophesied Messiah
of Daniel. And just to make sure, Rashi and his fellow
commentators really put the boot in by demoting the
book of Daniel from the prophetic canon.

We would be full of doubt and despair if it weren't for
the fact that the Masoretes weren't the only ones to
translate the book of Daniel from the original Hebrew.
Around seven centuries earlier Theodotion, a Jewish
scholar living in the Greek world, produced his own version, and it is his translation, without colon or *atnach*,

that forms the basis for the text used in the majority of Christian Bibles today. So the easy thing to say is that Theodotion got it right and the Masoretes got it wrong. Perhaps the Masoretes had an anti-Christian agenda? This is easy to say, but it is very wrong, because who are we to judge? What right do we have to comment on the work of these dedicated Jewish scholars, without whose work the Old Testament as we know it would never have appeared?

Praise God there is an answer. We can rest in our beds at night, our faith intact. There is a bigger story here. The Masoretes and Theodotion are both right. The *atnach* and other accents in that Daniel passage are there not only for grammatical but also for musical purposes. They are known as cantillation marks and there are more of them than there are letters in the English alphabet. Israel Yeivin, a Hebrew scholar and a leading Masoretic authority, wrote that the main function of the accents was '*to represent the musical motifs to which the Biblical text was chanted in the public reading.*'[6] The Daniel passage is littered with them, which at the very least should cast severe doubts on our pesky *atnach*. Is it a punctuation mark or is it a musical notation? The fact that it does not appear in the earlier translation by Theodotion speaks volumes. This provides us with reasonable doubt as to the exact reading of the verse, which is enough to throw out the whole case as unproven through lack of firm evidence. So what I am saying is that since we can't say for sure whether the notation was for musical or punctuation purposes, there is sufficient justification to read the verse without the distraction of the *atnach* and to feel secure in our Christian interpretation. After all, this was good enough for the early translations, the Septuagint and the Theodotion translation, without an *atnach* in sight.

> *'Know and understand this: From the issuing of the decree to restore and rebuild Jerusalem until the Anointed One, the ruler, comes, there will be seven "sevens", and sixty-two "sevens". It will be rebuilt with streets and a trench, but in times of trouble.'*

What an interesting story. I hope that I still have your attention. The *atnach* episode has been included for a purpose. It tells us that the truth will always out, but sometimes we must not give up but keep on digging. We must realize that the Hebrew scriptures are uniquely precious to Orthodox rabbis and they are hurt when they see untrained Christians extracting key verses, often out of context, to justify their belief in Jesus the Messiah. Their scholars have developed rebuttals to every proof text Christians may use, so it is a worthy exercise to enter their world and consider these responses. This is why we need to know the full story behind our *atnach* episode, so that we can thoroughly counter not just Jewish objections but also, it is sad to say, some Christian ones.

So the Promised One is to appear and to be killed around AD 33.

Every Sabbath in synagogues throughout the world, a portion of Scripture is read out from the Torah, the first five books of the Bible. The readings are part of a yearly cycle, ending every year at the celebration called *Simchat Torah*, after which the Torah scroll is rerolled and returned to Genesis 1.

In the service, after the Torah reading there is a second reading, from other Old Testament scriptures, mainly from the books of the Prophets. These are the *Haftarah* readings. There is a Christian urban legend that speaks of an anomaly in the cycle of Haftarah readings. It asserts that as part of the cycle, the complete book of Isaiah is read out, but that one portion is skipped. This is the portion that includes Isaiah 53, the famous Suffering Servant verses. The reasoning is that the Jewish religious authorities are so embarrassed that these verses speak of Jesus that they hide them away from their congregants in case they hear them and immediately get converted to Christianity!

Let's get real. There is a measure of truth here, but it's mixed up with some wild exaggerations. First, the annual cycle of Haftarah readings nowhere nearly covers all the books of the Prophets; in fact only just over a third of the book of Isaiah is covered. What is true, though, is that around September time there are subsequent weeks when Isaiah is covered. The first week, the *Shoftim* Torah reading, has Isaiah 51:12 – 52:12 as the Haftarah portion. The second week, the *Ki Tetse* Torah reading, has Isaiah 54:1–10 as the Haftarah portion. The verses that are skipped are Isaiah 52:13 – 53:12, the section that is labelled *The Suffering and Glory of the Servant* in your NIV Bible.

So it is true that our contentious section of Scripture is skipped over, but we could equally ask why the Haftarah readings are never taken from Isaiah chapters 2 – 5, 8, 10 – 26, 30 – 39, 45 – 48, 59, 64, 65 or 66.

Nit-picking aside, what really is so special about the section of Scripture known as *The Suffering and Glory of the Servant*? Well, we are quite familiar with some of the key verses. Here is a particularly familiar extract:

> *'Who has believed our message and to whom has the arm of the LORD been revealed? He grew up before him like a tender shoot, and like a root out of dry ground. He had no beauty or majesty to attract us to him, nothing in his appearance that we should*

desire him. He was despised and rejected by men, a man of sorrows, and familiar with suffering. Like one from whom men hide their faces he was despised, and we esteemed him not. Surely he took up our infirmities and carried our sorrows, yet we considered him stricken by God, smitten by him, and afflicted. But he was pierced for our transgressions, he was crushed for our iniquities; the punishment that brought us peace was upon him, and by his wounds we are healed. We all, like sheep, have gone astray, each of us has turned to his own way; and the LORD *has laid on him the iniquity of us all' (Is. 53:1–6).*

Our first task is to be absolutely clear about who this passage is referring to, rather than just saying, 'Oh yes, that's Jesus, isn't it?' We need to look at the context, in case we are 'conned by the text'. The passage is introduced in Isaiah 52:13, where the entity is called the *servant*. I am treading carefully here and even avoiding personalization (i.e. using the word 'entity' rather than 'person'), because those perceived fears of the Jewish religious establishment mentioned earlier are real fears after all. If this reference to the Suffering Servant could point to Jesus, as it seems to do in Christian eyes, then some open-minded Jews might start to recognize the Messiah here, rabbis forbid!

In the section of Isaiah from chapter 40 onwards, a *servant* is mentioned nineteen times, in the so-called Servant Songs, and we start to wonder whether these modern rabbis may have a point after all.

Isaiah 41:8 says, '*But you, O Israel, my servant, Jacob, whom I have chosen, you descendants of Abraham my friend.*'

Isaiah 44:1 says, '*But now listen, O Jacob, my servant, Israel, whom I have chosen.*'

Isaiah 44:21 says, '*Remember these things, O Jacob, for you are my servant, O Israel. I have made you, you are my servant; O Israel, I will not forget you.*'

Isaiah 45:4 says, '*For the sake of Jacob my servant, of Israel my chosen, I summon you by name and bestow on you a title of honour, though you do not acknowledge me.*'

In fact over half of the 'servant' verses clearly speak of the nation of Israel, or the Jewish people. This leads many modern religious Jewish commentators to suggest that our passage in Isaiah 53 is clearly referring to the Jewish people. If you read that passage again in the light of Jewish history you can see where they are coming from, but you also see some other things.

> '*Surely he took up our infirmities and carried our sorrows, yet we considered him stricken by God, smitten by him, and afflicted. But he was pierced for our transgressions, he was crushed for our iniquities; the punishment that brought us peace was upon him, and by his wounds we are healed. We all, like sheep, have gone astray, each of us has turned to his own way; and the LORD has laid on him the iniquity of us all.*'

So how *do* the Jewish people heal through their wounds or carry the iniquity of the world? They are hardly equipped to fulfil this holy role, as Isaiah tells us a little earlier in his prophecies:

> '*Ah, sinful nation, a people loaded with guilt, a brood of evildoers, children given to corruption! They have forsaken the LORD; they have spurned the Holy One of Israel and turned their backs on him*' (Is. 1:4).

It just doesn't scan that this people, no more or less sinful than any other people who have walked the earth, could fulfil the role of this Suffering Servant.

So we have to conclude that although earlier verses in Isaiah speak of Israel as the 'servant', the Suffering Servant of Isaiah 53 is an individual. A hint of his identity is given in Targum Jonathan on Isaiah 52:13:

> *'Behold, my servant, the Anointed One (Messiah) shall pros-*
> *per . . .'*

Those Jews living just after New Testament times, listening to this Targum read out in the synagogue, would have been in no doubt that the Suffering Servant is an individual, the Messiah, the Anointed One, and some of them would eventually realize that this very person, Jesus of Nazareth, had actually come. Many of them would realize that Jesus' life of service and death on the cross followed the script of Isaiah 52:13 – 53:12 to the letter, as well as much of Psalm 22. The Suffering Servant had come in the flesh and walked among them.

We have seen that according to contemporary Jewish opinion, the Suffering Servant was a role fulfilled by the Jewish people. It is significant to note that this wasn't always the opinion of Jewish sages through the ages, even of those living through the furnace of Christian anti-Jewish persecution. Of course the Targum identified the Suffering Servant with the Messiah himself, and this is the generally accepted view of all the early Jewish writings, including the Talmud, the Midrashim and the Zohar, and also of the highly revered rabbi Maimonides.

Despite what most modern rabbis may say, the Suffering Servant was certainly identified with the Messiah by earlier rabbis. In the sixteenth century Rabbi Don Yitzchak Abarbanel admitted,

> *'The first question is to ascertain to whom (this scripture)*
> *refers: for the learned among the Nazarenes expound it of the*
> *man who was crucified in Jerusalem at the end of the second*
> *temple and who according to them was the Son of God and*

> *took flesh in the virgin's womb as it is stated in their writings.*
> *Jonathan ben Uzziel interpreted it in the Targum of the future*
> *Messiah; but this is also the opinion of our learned men in the*
> *majority of the midrashim.'[7]*

Another sixteenth-century rabbi, Moshe Alshekh, stated:

> *'(Our) Rabbis with one voice accept and affirm the opinion*
> *that the prophet is speaking of king Messiah.'[8]*

> *'Rejoice greatly, O Daughter of Zion! Shout, Daughter of*
> *Jerusalem! See, your king comes to you, righteous and having*
> *salvation, gentle and riding on a donkey, on a colt, the foal of*
> *a donkey' (Zech. 9:9).*

This is a gentle individual with the key to salvation, and we know from our reading of the Gospel account of the triumphal entry to Jerusalem that Jesus was a perfect fulfilment of this (Mt. 21:5).

We conclude this little section by considering the episode of the apostle Philip and the Ethiopian eunuch in Acts 8:26–40. The eunuch was reading from the Suffering Servant verses in Isaiah 53 and needed to know who was being referred to here. In verse 35, Philip responds:

> *'Then Philip began with that very passage of Scripture and*
> *told him the good news about Jesus.'*

So the Promised One is to be born to servanthood and suffering.

The virgin birth of Jesus. On the one hand we have the Orthodox Jews, secularists and liberal Christians telling us to 'get a life' and stop believing in this impossible craziness. On the other, some traditional Catholics have stretched out the doctrine to the curious extreme of asserting that Mary stayed a virgin for the rest of her life, even after she gave birth to Jesus! Even more ridiculous is the news story that broke in 2006 of three Scottish sisters who had been insured since 2000 against the possibility of having a virgin birth. The payout would have been to cover the cost of caring and bringing up the Christ! There's nowt as mad as folk![9]

It's clearly a key doctrine. So where does the truth lie? Well, it lies in the content, context and interpretation of a single verse in Isaiah:

> 'Therefore the Lord himself will give you a sign: The virgin will be with child and will give birth to a son, and will call him Immanuel' (Is. 7:14).[10]

Jewish scholars have three objections to the idea that this verse is fulfilled by the virgin birth of Jesus. First, that the context indicates this verse was referring to events at the time of Isaiah; secondly, that it refers to a chap called Immanuel, not Jesus, and thirdly, that the original Hebrew does not refer to a virgin and the Christians have mistranslated it.

The context of the verse is Isaiah meeting up with the King of Judah, who was troubled by the threat from the Northern Kingdoms. Isaiah reassured him that the Lord would not let this happen and, to prove it, would supply a sign. A child would be born, and before he came of age the threats would be no more, in fact the Northern Kingdoms would be laid waste themselves.

You can hear the objections. *So this child was surely born normally. And how could Christians dare to take this verse out of context and read into it an event far off in the future?*

To answer this, first read chapter 7 of Isaiah for your-self, paying particular attention to the Hebrew grammar. Of course, we are reading an English translation from the original Hebrew, so you are going to have to take my word for it. The fact is that this passage contains two sep-arate prophecies, for two different groups of people. The reason we know this is through investigating the Hebrew grammar, in particular the use of *singular* and *plural* words. Without going into complex detail on this, when Isaiah is talking to the king the words are in the *singular*, but in verses 13 and 14 he is speaking in the *plural*, to the house of David. So we can envisage the scene. Isaiah is attempting to prophesy to the king, who is being obstruc-tive, so he moves the focus away from the king, uttering an awesome prophecy to the house of David, Jewish peo-ple in general, speaking of a future man, born of a virgin. Having made this proclamation, he returns to the present, finishing his word to the king. So, two prophecies were given: an immediate one to the king, related to his current concerns, and a future one to the house of David.

Having covered the context, we move to the most crit-ical point of contention: does the Hebrew word *almah*, used in this passage, translate as 'virgin' or 'maiden'? The only other occurrences of this word in Scripture, in Genesis 24:43, Proverbs 30:19, Psalm 68:25, Song of Songs 1:3 and Song of Songs 6:8–9, all make more sense translated as 'virgin'. So it is perfectly reasonable for us to do so here, too. Let's return to our verse.

> *'Therefore the Lord himself will give you a sign: The virgin will be with child and will give birth to a son, and will call him Immanuel' (Is. 7:14).*

The word used for 'sign' here, *ot*, always refers to a gen-uine supernatural miracle. It appears in Exodus, when

Moses' rod becomes a serpent and his hand leprous. It is also the word used when the sun's shadow changes direction as a sign to King Hezekiah. So the scene is set. The Lord's sign is going to be a supernatural event, a true miracle. A virgin birth certainly fits the bill: any other translation of *almah* does not speak of anything more than a commonplace occurrence – after all, there's nothing special about an ordinary lady producing a son and then naming him. Further evidence is provided in the translation of the Hebrew scriptures into Greek by Jewish scholars in the third century BC, the *Septuagint*. They translated *almah* as *parthenos*, a Greek word that only has the meaning of 'virgin', with no axe to grind, as Jesus wasn't to appear for hundreds of years. This brings us to a clincher, an argument provided by the Jewish critics themselves. If, as they say, the Gospel writers fabricated their accounts by declaring the virgin birth of Jesus a mark of his Messiahship, there must have been an expectation in the first century that the Messiah would be born of a virgin and not just any young maiden.

But 'Jesus'? *Surely he was to be named 'Immanuel'*, the critics cry. I must admit, this had troubled me too, particularly when reading from the Matthew account:

> 'She will give birth to a son, and you are to give him the name
> Jesus, because he will save his people from their sins' (Mt. 1:21).

Yes, he is to be called *Jesus*. Then we are reminded, in the next verses:

> 'All this took place to fulfil what the Lord had said through the
> prophet: "The virgin will be with child and will give birth to a
> son, and they will call him Immanuel" – which means, "God
> with us."'

Immanuel or Jesus? Which is it to be? The answer is . . . both! This is one of the beauties of Hebraic thought. Names are not just names. They are intended to have meaning. The Bible is full of this concept. Virtually everyone in the Bible has a name that describes something relevant about that person or the situation in which he or she found themselves. From Adam (Hebrew for 'man') to Zechariah ('God has remembered'), we have a cast of thousands of colourful characters. Then, of course, Jesus is our 'Man of Many Names', with over 350 names, each describing an aspect of his nature or mission. The name 'Jesus' means 'God is salvation'. As he chiefly came to save the world, surely it is apt that his given name reflects that fact. Immanuel, as the Gospel account tells us, means 'God with us', a comfort to us all, but still not a name with the power of Jesus, our Saviour. We could call him Immanuel, Son of Man, Son of God, the Word or Messiah, but it's far more convenient to call him by the name his mum and dad were told by an angel to give him, Jesus, or *Yeshua* in Hebrew.

So the Promised One is to be born of a virgin.

We have just gone through what are probably the three contentious areas, the three scriptures fulfilled by Jesus that religious Jews have the most trouble with. But there are others that I will now deal with briefly, with some food for thought rather than a comprehensive analysis:

> 'For to us a child is born, to us a son is given, and the government will be on his shoulders. And he will be called Wonderful Counsellor, Mighty God, Everlasting Father, Prince of Peace. Of the increase of his government and peace there will be no end. He will reign on David's throne and over his kingdom, establishing and upholding it with justice and righteousness

from that time on and for ever. The zeal of the LORD *Almighty
will accomplish this' (Is. 9:6–7).*

A standard Jewish response to this is that these titles do
not refer to Jesus, as he was never called by any of them
during his lifetime. Actually, that's not the point, as
these titles are names given to both God and the
Promised One himself in Jewish writings. It is clear that
this is a reference to the Promised One, as he will *reign
on David's throne*, a necessary condition for Messiahship.
So this passage could be paraphrased, '*For to us a child is
born . . . and he will be God Himself . . .*' The point is not
that this couldn't be a specific reference to Jesus, but that
if Jesus has a claim to be the Promised One, he would
also need to be God Himself.

These titles are known as the 'throne names' of the
Messiah, the Promised One. Jewish commentators generally state that these titles belong either to God Himself
or to a Jewish contemporary – King Hezekiah is the
usual suspect. But Ibn Ezra, one of the greatest biblical
commentators of all, refused to follow the party line and
stated explicitly that these were all the names of this
child of the future – this child who would grow up to be
the man who would be God.

So the Promised One would be God Himself.

> '*But you, Bethlehem Ephrathah, though you are small among
> the clans of Judah, out of you will come for me one who will be
> ruler over Israel, whose origins are from of old, from ancient
> times' (Mich. 5:2).*

Reading this verse in its entirety, we are looking for a
Promised One who had existed from long before. This is
a reference to the *Memra*, the manifestation of Jesus at

the time of Creation. There is further affirmation of this in the Targum Jonathan:

> '*And You Bethlehem Ephrath, you who were too small to be numbered among the thousands of the house of Judah, from you shall come forth before Me The Messiah, to exercise dominion over Israel, He whose name was mentioned from before, from the Days of Creation.*'

The Messiah, who was also the *Memra*, was to be born in Bethlehem. It is most unlikely that any Messiah is going to come out of present-day Bethlehem, as today it is an Arab town with not a Jew to be seen.

So the Promised One would be born in Bethlehem.

You should now have a reasonable portrait of the Promised One. Yet the battle for truth is ongoing, and although I have presented, I believe, a reasonable apologetic for Jesus as the fulfilment, the opposition will never be satisfied until the Holy Spirit illuminates their heart. We can only go so far in our debates, whether over prophecy fulfilment or over any number of battle-grounds, ranging from the very existence of God to issues of Creation, Israel or the end-times. In the final analysis it is all a matter of faith. You either believe or you don't. You either want to believe or you find yourself in opposition for reasons that perhaps you are not even clear about. But if you are a believer in Jesus, this chapter shows you that in the great debates of biblical interpretation we do have reasonable answers for the Christian position. We must not feel insecure when confronted by alternative explanations. The fact is that whatever answer we give will always be queried and challenged, but at least we are providing food for thought.

There can only be one truth, and although religious Jews may think they are fighting the good fight by defending traditions that have been handed down to them, there are no better weapons than an open mind and an open and willing heart prepared for change, however painful.

Notes

[1] Megillah 14a.

[2] Rashi's commentary on Megillah 3a.

[3] Rashi's commentary on Sanhedrin 2.

[4] These calculations are covered in many other books and websites on this subject. A good place to start is Chuck Missler's article and mp3 download at http://www.khouse.org/articles/2004/552/.

[5] *Inspiration and Canonicity of the Bible: An Historical and Exegetical Study, Contemporary Evangelical Perspectives*, 2nd ed. (Grand Rapids: Zondervan, 1969), p. 58.

[6] Israel Yeivin, 'Introduction to the Tiberian Masorah', trans. and ed. by E. J. Revell, *Society of Biblical Literature Masoretic Studies*, No 5 (Missoula, MT: Scholars Press, 1980), p. 158.

[7] Arnold Fruchtenbaum, *Jesus was a Jew* (Ariel Ministries, 1981), p. 26.

[8] Rachmiel Frydland, *What the Rabbis know about the Messiah* (Messianic Publishing Co., 1985), p. 53.

[9] http://news.bbc.co.uk/1/hi/scotland/highlands_and_islands/5105946.stm

[10] For a fuller discussion of this topic I recommend you read Chapter 6 of Tony Pearce's *The Messiah Factor* (New Wine Press, 2004).

PART TWO

The Incarnation

4

Yeshua ben Yosef

Question: How Jewish was Jesus?

Picture the scene. It's two thousand years ago, in a small
village called Nazareth, in the Galilee region of what is
now the land of Israel. You see a little boy playing in the
backyard among the wood piles and shavings. His
father, Yosef, is in the workshop next to the yard and his
mother, Miriam, is busy cooking. His name is *Yeshua ben
Yosef*. You know him better as Jesus, son of Joseph.

It is time for lunch and his mother calls him. If Miriam
had called him by the name 'Jesus', two things would
have happened. First, he would have carried on playing,
not recognizing the command, and secondly, the neighbours would have been astonished at Miriam's bad
attempt at Greek, a feat which was about as likely as your
average cockney walking up to a pub landlord and asking for a pint of beer in his best classical Latin. If she'd
added the epithet 'Christ', the situation would have been
even more dramatic, because not only would he have
continued to ignore her and the neighbours been astonished at her Greek, but she would also have been stoned
to death for assigning a forbidden and blasphemous title

to her son. That is because 'Christ', the English version of *Christos*, is the Greek translation of the Hebrew word *Mashiach*, which means 'Messiah', or 'anointed one'. And no Jew would dare to make a claim to that title. Well, not until this particular boy became a man and embarked on his life's mission.

Yeshua (Jesus) was a nice Jewish boy, who any mother would be proud of. He was born in Bethlehem, as the Christmas cards show us, in very humble surroundings. After birth he had been circumcised and consecrated at the temple and, by all accounts, had the typical childhood of one from a poor family in a Galilean village. And how do we know they were poor? 'No room at the inn' was certainly a clue, but the clincher was the *'pair of doves or two young pigeons'* that they sacrificed to the Lord after the birth. This was the *pidyon ha-Ben*, the redemption of a boy. It's an acknowledgement that every first-born boy belongs to God and his parents must 'buy him back' by making a sacrifice. This rule dated right back to the time of Moses, when the first-born boys of the Israelites were spared from the Angel of Death on Passover night. Joseph and Mary were too poor to offer a lamb sacrifice and so were permitted to offer up the birds as a cheaper alternative.

They were poor, but they must have been devout Jews. Not all families made the annual pilgrimage to Jerusalem, but Luke 2:41 tells us:

> *'Every year his parents went to Jerusalem for the Feast of the Passover.'*

For poor people this was exceptional, and it tells us that God indeed made the correct choice in parents for Yeshua. Another clue is in the song, the Magnificat, sung by Miriam (Mary) when she visited her relative

Elizabeth. This song alludes to no less than thirteen Hebrew scriptures, telling us that even at a relatively young age the mother of Yeshua was fully conversant with the Judaism of her day.

But what of Yeshua and his education? The Mishnah, a third-century collection of the oral 'Traditions of the Elders', tells us that Jewish boys of the day would study the Torah (the first five books of the Bible) at the age of 5 and the oral 'Traditions' at the age of 10, and be trained in *halachot*, rabbinic legal decisions, at the ripe old age of 15.[1] Sunday School was never harder! It was made more difficult still when one realizes that reading material was scarce and a poor family like theirs would have, at best, just one or two biblical scrolls, just a small part of the total breadth of Scripture. Much, therefore, was committed to memory. In the schools, study of the Bible was often done by chanting aloud. In that day people passing by such schools would remark on 'the chirping of children'.[2]

The Talmud sheds some light on techniques used to commit Scripture to memory by describing the mnemonics used to teach small children the Hebrew alphabet.[3] Children used the Sabbath day of rest to memorize material learnt in the week.[4] And if they ventured outside while memorizing, there was a warning in the Mishnah:

> *'A person walking along the road repeating his lessons who interrupts his memorization and exclaims: "What a beautiful tree!" or "What a beautiful field!" it is imputed to him as if he were guilty of a crime punishable by death.'*[5]

The Talmud also sings the praises of memorization:

> *'A person who repeats his lesson a hundred times is not to be compared to a person who repeats it a hundred and one times.'*[6]

*'If a student learns Torah and does not go over it again and
again, he is like a man who sows without reaping.'*[7]

It was a serious business being a first-century Jewish
schoolkid! So what was Yeshua doing in those silent
early years? He was hard at study, memorizing Scripture
and rabbinical commentary, in common with most other
Jewish youths of his day. By the time he had left his ado-
lescent years he would have memorized most of the
written Torah. From then on his mother kept one eye on
him, as he *'grew in wisdom and stature, and in favour with
God and men'*.

The boy became a man as Yeshua arrived by the banks
of the river Jordan, where his relative, John the Baptist
(Yochanan the Immerser), was 'preparing the way'.
'Baptise me,' said Yeshua. *'You've got to be kidding!'*
responded John. *'Do I look like I'm kidding? Let it be so!'*
The act of baptism, was, in the words of Alfred
Edersheim, 'the last act of his private life'.[8] This was
some beginning to this unique and awesome ministry.
Heaven opens and the Spirit of God descends like a
dove, and a voice from heaven proclaims, *'This is my
Son, whom I love; with him I am well pleased,'* a combina-
tion of Psalm 2:7 and Isaiah 42:1. The common interpretation of the symbolism here is that it is an expression of
the Trinity: God the Father commending God the Son in
the presence of God the Holy Spirit, who takes the form
of a dove.

Yeshua began his ministry. His deeds may have been
mighty, but in appearance he was just like any other
Jewish itinerant teacher. Far from the blue-eyed, chisel-
jawed Hollywood Swede, or the dreamy fair-haired
Renaissance Italian, he was an olive-skinned, dark-
haired first-century Jew. The Samaritan woman certainly
thought so.

> 'The Samaritan woman said to him, "You are a Jew and I am a Samaritan woman"' (*Jn. 4:9*).

He certainly dressed as a religious Jew. A clue is in this passage:

> 'Just then a woman who had been subject to bleeding for twelve years came up behind him and touched the edge of his cloak. She said to herself, "If I only touch his cloak, I will be healed"' (*Mt. 9:20–21*).

It's not an obvious clue, because the translation does the original event no favour at all. The clue becomes clearer when we look at the same passage in the Jewish New Testament translation:

> 'A woman who had had a haemorrhage for twelve years approached him from behind and touched the tzitzit on his robe.'

Spot the strange word? *Tzitzit*. Some translations refer to it as a 'hem', which is only marginally more accurate than 'edge'. A better word is 'fringe' or 'tassel', a word that appears in Numbers 15:37–39:

> 'The LORD said to Moses, "Speak to the Israelites and say to them: 'Throughout the generations to come you are to make tassels on the corners of your garments, with a blue cord on each tassel. You will have these tassels to look at and so you will remember all the commands of the LORD, that you may obey them and not prostitute yourselves by going after the lusts of your own hearts and eyes.'"'

And that is what Jesus was wearing. A robe, like the garments worn by today's Bedouin, with tassels, or tzitzits, on each corner. It marked him out not just a Jew, but one who followed the Torah and lived by it, as directed by that passage in Numbers.

He taught in synagogues and the Jewish temple, without a Gentile in sight. Much of his teaching was in a thoroughly Jewish context, as we will see in Chapter 6. He visited Jerusalem for the pilgrim feasts of *Pesach*[10] (Passover), *Shavuot*[11] (Pentecost) and *Succot*[12] (Tabernacles), as well as *Chanukah*[13] (Dedication of the Temple) and made great use of their symbolism in his teachings, particularly when speaking of his mission on earth. He took great pains to affirm the major themes of the Old Testament, the only holy scriptures available to the Jews of his day.

There is a good way of grasping this important point, and that is by showing the connection between Yeshua and a key character from the Hebrew scriptures. The link is a prophecy in Deuteronomy:

> 'The LORD your God will raise up for you a prophet like me from among your own brothers. You must listen to him. For this is what you asked of the LORD your God at Horeb on the day of the assembly when you said, "Let us not hear the voice of the LORD our God nor see this great fire anymore, or we will die." The LORD said to me: "What they say is good. I will raise up for them a prophet like you from among their brothers; I will put my words in his mouth, and he will tell them everything I command him. If anyone does not listen to my words that the prophet speaks in my name, I myself will call him to account"' (Deut. 18:15–19).

Who is God speaking to? It is Moses himself. Let's hear what Stephen had to say just before his stoning:

> 'For Moses said, "The Lord your God will raise up for you a prophet like me from among your own people; you must listen

*to everything he tells you. Anyone who does not listen to him
will be completely cut off from among his people." Indeed, all
the prophets from Samuel on, as many as have spoken, have
foretold these days' (Acts 3:22–24).*

Who is Stephen speaking about? None other than Jesus,
the *second* Moses.

In the religious Jewish community there is none more
revered than Moses. He is the giver of the Torah, the
deliverer from Egyptian bondage, the leader through the
wilderness, the miracle-maker of the Old Covenant.
When we look at the life and ministry of Jesus, we see
astonishing parallels:

- Both were born into a Hebrew world under Gentile
  domination (Egyptian and Roman)
- Both had unusual cots at birth (basket and man-
  ger)
- Both were saved from death at the king's order
  (Pharaoh, Herod)
- Both were raised in the home of one who was not
  their father (Pharaoh, Joseph)
- Both had to put up with criticism and persecution
  from their own people
- Both appointed seventy chosen helpers (Num. 11:16,
  Lk. 10:1)
- Both sent out twelve men on special missions (Num.
  13:1–2, Mt. 10:1,5)
- Both experienced forty-day fasts (Ex. 34:28, Mt. 4:1–2)
- Both fed multitudes by miraculous means (manna
  and quail, bread and fish)
- Both were touched by God so that their faces shone
  (Ex. 34:29–30, Mt. 17:1–2)
- Both heard God as an audible voice (Ex. 19:9,19, Jn.
  12:23,27–28)

- Both acted as mediators of a covenant that was sealed by blood (Ex. 24:7–8, Mt. 26:26–28)
- Both interceded for their people with God (Num. 11:1–2, Lk. 23:33–34)
- Both delivered their people from bondage (Ex. 3:9–10, Acts 7:25)
- Both performed miracles (Ex. 3:20, Jn. 5:19–20)
- Both appeared after death (transfiguration, resurrection)

This surely is enough to demonstrate the continuity between the Old and New Covenants. But we need to return to the prophecy given to Moses and decide whether Yeshua did indeed fulfil it.

> 'The LORD your God will raise up for you a prophet like me from among your own brothers . . .'

Was Yeshua *this* prophet? Let's examine further.

It's interesting that if you do a web search for 'prophet Jesus', the majority of hits are Muslim websites, or Christian websites speaking to Muslims. Muslims have no problems with considering Jesus (Yeshua) as prophet: it's the other stuff they take issue with! It's even more interesting to note that Jewish scholars of modern times have no problem with Yeshua as prophet: again, it's the other stuff they take issue with!

Yeshua certainly considered himself a prophet:

> 'Jesus said to them, "Only in his home town, among his relatives and in his own house is a prophet without honour"' (Mk. 6:4).

> 'In any case, I must keep going today and tomorrow and the next day – for surely no prophet can die outside Jerusalem!' (Lk. 13:33).

As did individuals who he ministered to:

> *'Sir,' the woman said, 'I can see that you are a prophet' (Jn. 4:19).*

> *'Finally they turned again to the blind man, "What have you to say about him? It was your eyes he opened." The man replied, "He is a prophet"' (Jn. 9:17).*

And so did the people . . .

> *'The crowds answered, "This is Jesus, the prophet from Nazareth in Galilee"' (Mt. 21:11).*

> *'They looked for a way to arrest him, but they were afraid of the crowd because the people held that he was a prophet' (Mt. 21:46).*

> *'They were all filled with awe and praised God. "A great prophet has appeared among us," they said. "God has come to help his people"' (Lk. 7:16).*

In Yeshua's day, before he had a chance to show them otherwise, there was a conviction that prophecy had ceased. There were no prophets in the vein of the Old Testament giants such as Isaiah or Jeremiah. The only prophetic expectation was for the return of Elijah and the coming of the Messiah, the awaited Prophet mentioned earlier. This is demonstrated first by a question posed to John the Baptist:

> *'They asked him, "Then who are you? Are you Elijah?" He said, "I am not." "Are you the Prophet?" He answered, "No"' (Jn. 1:21).*

And after Yeshua had been observed for some time by the Jews of his day, this was their conclusion:

> *'After the people saw the miraculous sign that Jesus did, they begin to say, "Surely this is the Prophet who is to come into the world"' (Jn. 6:14).*

> *'On hearing his words, some of the people said, "Surely this man is the Prophet"' (Jn. 7:40).*

As the only prophet awaited was the one prophesied by Moses, it seems that Yeshua, through his words and actions, fitted the bill, filled the vacancy.

> *'The LORD said to me: "What they say is good. I will raise up for them a prophet like you from among their brothers; I will put my words in his mouth, and he will tell them everything I command him. If anyone does not listen to my words that the prophet speaks in my name, I myself will call him to account"' (Deut. 18:17–19).*

Yeshua demonstrated this further by indicating exactly where his words came from:

> *'Jesus answered, "My teaching is not my own. It comes from him who sent me. If anyone chooses to do God's will, he will find out whether my teaching comes from God or whether I speak on my own"' (Jn. 7:16–17).*

> *'For I did not speak of my own accord, but the Father who sent me commanded me what to say and how to say it' (Jn. 12:49).*

Yeshua (Jesus) the Jew, the Prophet, the spokesperson for God Almighty, the man. I emphasize the latter, because the church has at times struggled with the idea of the humanity of Yeshua, the idea that God could walk this earth as a fully flesh-and-blood human being. To understand why, one needs some grasp of Greek philosophy, the prevalent mindset of the early church once it had jettisoned all traces of its true roots in the biblical, Hebraic mindset.

It can be traced back to Alexandria, Egypt, in the third century AD, when Christian theology was shaped by ideas handed down from such figures as the Greek philosopher Plato.

The problem is that the Greek thinking of the time could not get a handle on the concept of 'the Word becoming flesh', as stated at the start of John's Gospel. For them, everything material, such as the human body, was basically evil and the creation of an inferior god, whereas anything spiritual was basically good and the creation of a better god. Out of this craziness came an idea known as Docetism, taken from the Greek word for 'to seem'.

For followers of this heresy, Jesus only *appeared* to have a physical body, only appeared to eat and drink and talk and sleep and excrete bodily wastes. And if you have trouble considering the latter, then perhaps you, too, are a closet Docetist. That may seem a facetious comment, but it just shows you how ingrained these Greek ideas are in the current Christian psyche. The Hebraic and biblical view of our human existence is a holistic one, a seamless unity of mind, body and spirit. All are good and beneficial to our well-being. There's nothing crude and un-godlike about our bodily functions.

> 'Blessed be the LORD God, King of the Universe, who has created humans with wisdom, with openings and hollow parts, revealed before Your holy throne, that if any part of the body was to malfunction, it would be impossible for us to exist and stand before You even for a short time. You cure all flesh and perform wonders!'

Yes, this is the Jewish prayer for going to the toilet. Everything in life is a gift from God. Going to the toilet regularly is a blessing (to some more than others), no more or less than eating or receiving an answered prayer. All aspects of life should be the subject of thanks and all are present in the Jewish liturgy.

But the Greek Docetists weren't interested in the Jewish liturgy; they had rejected that long before, replacing it with the pagan ideas from Greek philosophy. For them, *Yeshua* was no more human than Spiderman or Dan Dare. For them, God could never take physical form, because matter and flesh were evil, so he could only *seem* to have a body, he could only *seem* to be crucified, could only *seem* to be resurrected.

Utter rubbish. Try telling that to Simon Peter, who ate fish with him, or the woman who poured oil over him. Try telling that to the hundreds of Jews who met him in his lifetime. Try telling that to Mary who gave birth to him: tell her that her contractions were just an illusion!

Joking aside, this episode shows how the truth can be the first victim when you are enslaved to an alien philosophy. The greatest error of the early Christian church was the decision to extract itself from the Jewish roots of the faith. The reasons for this are complex and are treated in depth in my books *The Land of Many Names* and *The People of Many Names*, but suffice it to say, invisible strings were pulled by the one who would seek to destroy all people of God.

Notes

1. Avot 5:21.
2. Patricia Hitchcock, *The Jewish People in the First Century* (Fortress, 1976), 2:953.

[3] Babylonian Talmud, Shabbat 104a.

[4] *The Jewish People in the First Century*, 2:954.

[5] Avot 3:8.

[6] Hagigah 9b.

[7] Sanhedrin 99a.

[8] Alfred Edersheim, *The Life and Times of Jesus the Messiah* (Hendrickson, 1993), Book 2, Chapter 12, p. 281.

[9] Berachoth 53b.

[10] Lk. 2:41, Jn. 2:13, Mt. 26:17.

[11] Although it is not stated explicitly, as a religious Jew he would have made a pilgrimage to Jerusalem for this feast. Of course it was on one such occasion that the Holy Spirit visited in power, Acts 2.

[12] Jn. 7:10.

[13] Jn. 10:22.

5

Christ

*Question: What exactly did Jesus do to make the
religious leaders so angry?*

They were not a happy folk. Decades of military occupation by a procession of foreign powers came at a time
when their holy men had been strangely silent, as if their
God had gone on vacation to another planet. For the
Jews this period had lasted for around four hundred
years and it was no joke. For a people who had experienced the glories of the days of the former kings, the current indignities of the Roman cosh were hard to bear.
They dreamt of better days. They dreamt of a Messiah, a
charismatic leader, who was going to free them from the
shackles of the Roman occupation, perhaps another
Joshua or David. But who would be this Messiah, and
how would he go about his master plan for ejecting
those unwanted tourists?

So the impression seems to be that Jesus was a most
unexpected candidate for the vacancy of a macho-liber-
ating-freedom-fighter-type-of-messiah that the Jews
under savage Roman occupation longed for. They wanted a Barabbas (whose name curiously translates as 'son

of the father'). They yearned for a lion but received a lamb. Expectations were high when Jesus appeared on the scene, on account of Daniel's pinpoint prediction, as explained in Chapter 3. The Magi from the east, who would have had access to the book of Daniel, written as it was in eastern lands during the exile in Babylon, could read the signs of the times. Why else would they have embarked on that hazardous journey to a country ruled by that *meshuggenah* king, Herod? The atmosphere was so rich in Messianic hope, you could feel it in every pore of your body.

As we have already discussed, a good way to build an authentic story of Jesus is to find out which Bible verses cause the most controversy to Jewish critics. In this chapter we are going to examine Jesus' claims to be the Messiah of the Jews, so it's worth now looking through the Jewish and Christian scriptures and reading the script first.

If you do a computer word search of the Bible on the word 'Messiah' you are going to be disappointed and puzzled. You will not find any mentions of it at all in the Old Testament and only two inclusions in the New Testament. Since these two are not self-proclamations by Jesus himself but rather declarations by the disciple Andrew and the Samaritan woman, Jewish critics exclaim, '*Hey, he didn't even call himself the Messiah!*' This is a bogus remark, as you can use the same argument to declare that as the word 'Messiah' doesn't appear at all in the Old Testament, the whole concept is non-biblical!

Instead, we need to get back to basics. In the Old Testament, the expression you should have searched on was 'anointed one'. You'll find over forty mentions here, and you'll find that in most cases it is referring to a named individual. Usually it is a king of Israel: in most cases King David, but also Saul, Solomon, Joash,

Jehoahaz and Jehu. This makes sense, as a Jewish king would be anointed with oil for service, making him an *anointed one*.

> *'Then the men of Judah came to Hebron and there they anointed David king over the house of Judah' (2 Sam. 2:4).*

Then there are a couple of mentions of prophets, a foreign king, Cyrus of Persia, and even an allusion to Satan in Ezekiel 28:14.

But there are four instances of 'anointed one' that refer to an individual who is not named:

> *'I will raise up for myself a faithful priest, who will do according to what is in my heart and mind. I will firmly establish his house, and he will minister before my **anointed one** always' (1 Sam. 2:35).*

> *'The kings of the earth take their stand and the rulers gather together against the* LORD *and against his **Anointed One*** *(Ps. 2:2).*

> *'The Spirit of the Sovereign* LORD *is on me, because the* LORD *has **anointed** me to preach good news to the poor. He has sent me to bind up the broken-hearted, to proclaim freedom for the captives and release from darkness for the prisoners' (Is. 61:1).*

> *'Know and understand this: From the issuing of the decree to restore and rebuild Jerusalem until the **Anointed One**, the ruler, comes, there will be seven "sevens", and sixty-two "sevens". It will be rebuilt with streets and a trench, but in times of trouble' (Dan. 9:25).*

If you now look up these verses in the original Hebrew (as you do), you will find that the word translated as 'anointed one' is *mashiach*, transliterated into English as 'Messiah'.

So, in terms of a wait for a special person, an unnamed 'anointed one' or Messiah, there are only four relevant verses. I find this amazing, because when we look at the above verses, only two of them are specific. One, the Daniel verse examined in Chapter 3, indicates when this Messiah is to arrive on the earth, and the other, the Isaiah verse, gives an insight into his character. There are no other instances in the Old Testament where the Messiah (anointed one) is specifically spoken of. This is mind-blowing.

To be pedantic, the 'Messiah' that the Jews speak of, the conquering king, is never described as an 'anointed one' in Scripture. The *anointed* one of Daniel 9:25 is no conquering king. The only place where we are provided with a definition of this Messiah, in terms of what he's actually going to do, is in Isaiah 61:1:

> 'The Spirit of the Sovereign LORD is on me, because the LORD has anointed me to preach good news to the poor. He has sent me to bind up the broken-hearted, to proclaim freedom for the captives and release from darkness for the prisoners' (Is. 61:1).

This is chillingly exciting when we consider the one individual who, in what was possibly his first public outing in his home synagogue, did the following:

> 'He went to Nazareth, where he had been brought up, and on the Sabbath day he went into the synagogue, as was his custom. And he stood up to read. The scroll of the prophet Isaiah was handed to him. Unrolling it, he found the place where it is written: "The Spirit of the Lord is on me, because he has anointed me to preach good news to the poor. He has sent me to proclaim freedom for the prisoners and recovery of sight for

> *the blind, to release the oppressed, to proclaim the year of the*
> LORD'S *favour"' (Lk. 4:16–19).*

This man was, of course, Jesus, and in Luke 4:18-19 he identified himself with the only Old Testament scripture that spoke specifically and overtly of the Messiah. What I am saying here is that with just two verses from the Old Testament we can create a pretty good case for Jesus fulfilling the role of Messiah. How wonderful is that?

Returning to our computer word search, we can easily address the Jewish objection that Jesus never referred to himself as Messiah with what we have just learnt. But we can go further. Our search of the Old Testament yielded zero results with the English transliteration 'Messiah' but hit the button with the original Hebrew words 'anointed one', and we will find the same happens with the New Testament. As the New Testament was originally written in Greek, if we search on the word more identified with the Greek than with the Hebrew we are more likely to get results. That word is, of course, 'Christ'. When the New Testament writers translated from spoken Hebrew into Greek, they looked for the word that would best fit the translation of 'anointed one'. That word was *Christos*. When the English translators created our New Testament from the original Greek, they simply substituted the word 'Christ' for *Christos*. It is interesting to see that in the only two verses in the New Testament that include the word Messiah, in both cases (Jn. 1:41 and Jn. 4:25), the word 'Christ' is added in brackets afterwards!

A word search for 'Christ' in the New Testament provides 531 results. Of these, the following should be sufficient evidence that Jesus was identified with the 'anointed one', or Messiah, or Christ, spoken of in Isaiah 61:1:

'Then he warned his disciples not to tell anyone that he was the Christ' (Mt. 16:20).

'But Jesus remained silent. The high priest said to him, "I charge you under oath by the living God: Tell us if you are the Christ, the Son of God"' (Mt. 26:63).

'So when the crowd had gathered, Pilate asked them, "Which one do you want me to release to you: Barabbas, or Jesus who is called Christ?"' (Mt. 27:17).

'I tell you the truth, anyone who gives you a cup of water in my name because you belong to Christ will certainly not lose his reward' (Mk. 9:41).

'"Let this Christ, this King of Israel, come down now from the cross, that we may see and believe." Those crucified with him also heaped insults on him' (Mk. 15:32).

'Did not the Christ have to suffer these things and then enter his glory?' (Lk. 24:26).

'He told them, "This is what is written: The Christ will suffer and rise from the dead on the third day"' (Lk. 24:46).

'"Yes, Lord," she told him, "I believe that you are the Christ, the Son of God, who was to come into the world"' (Jn. 11:27).

The real clincher is the following verse, the only time he referred to himself as Jesus Christ, Jesus the Anointed One:

'Now this is eternal life: that they may know you, the only true God, and Jesus Christ, whom you have sent' (Jn. 17:3).

This is in his great prayer for himself, where he summarizes his mission so far and prepares himself for the next, and final, stage of his life on earth.

So, to rewind to the beginning of our story, we read of Jesus, at the very start of his ministry, arriving that Sabbath at his home synagogue in Nazareth, a place where he and his family would have been known and loved. After the customary reading from the Torah, Jesus was called up to read the Haftarah, verses from the Ketuvim (writings) and Nevi'im (prophets). He stood up for the set reading for that week, taken from Isaiah 61, verses 1 and 2, then sat down, according to the rabbinic custom, and for the first time in his home synagogue – to people who had watched him grow from child to youth and to man – began to preach, starting with the words, *'Today this scripture is fulfilled in your hearing.'*

By doing so he cemented the heart of God into time and place. Here was Jesus, identifying with the promised Messiah of Isaiah 61 and announcing that the time had come for its fulfilment. But perhaps the penny didn't quite drop yet . . .

The young man started well. *'All spoke well of him and were amazed at the gracious words that came from his lips'* (Lk. 4:22). They were perhaps amazed at the eloquence and the style of delivery. *Isn't this Joseph's son? Doesn't he speak well? A credit to his parents!* Joseph, the humble carpenter (if still alive), must have beamed as he sat in the congregation. Then the sermon took an unexpected turn.

There was evidently a back story here. His reputation was not unknown to his friends and family in Nazareth, as he had already taught in other synagogues and had been praised for it. He had also demonstrated his calling through various healings, notably one in nearby Capernaum that remains unrecorded. So the initial positive vibes as he started his sermon in Nazareth were to be expected.

Then the bombshell. The penny dropped. This man meant business and was not going to mince his words just because he was with friends and family.

> *'Jesus said to them, "Surely you will quote this proverb to me: 'Physician, heal yourself! Do here in your home town what we have heard that you did in Capernaum'"' (Lk. 4:23).*

What was this? It seems there were expectations here that Jesus had no intention of fulfilling. He was his own man; he was God's man (and man's God!).

But he was also the promised Messiah, and one of the first things he did was to prove it, without a shadow of a doubt, to the religious authorities of his day. He was going to fulfil the divine mandate, as prophesied by Isaiah and proclaimed by Jesus in his home synagogue:

> *'The Spirit of the Lord is on me, because he has anointed me to preach good news to the poor. He has sent me to proclaim freedom for the prisoners and recovery of sight for the blind, to release the oppressed, to proclaim the year of the Lord's favour.'*

He was going to preach the good news to the poor. He was going to proclaim freedom for the prisoners, including healing for the blind. He was also going to release the oppressed. It would truly be the year of the Lord's favour.

His miracles were going to have a significant purpose, particularly those performed early in his ministry in the Galilee area. If the promised Messiah was going to *proclaim freedom for prisoners*, there could not have been an imprisonment much worse than the death sentence of

leprosy. So healing a person with leprosy would certainly cause a stir. Having leprosy was real bad news.
Talking to someone with the disease was almost as bad;
in fact you were meant to stay at least six feet away.
Touching such a person was considered sheer madness,
so Jesus certainly made an impression when he met,
touched and healed a man with leprosy who
approached him.

> *'While Jesus was in one of the towns, a man came along
> who was covered with leprosy. When he saw Jesus, he fell
> with his face to the ground and begged him, "Lord, if you
> are willing, you can make me clean." Jesus reached out his
> hand and touched the man. "I am willing," he said. "Be
> clean!" And immediately the leprosy left him'* (Lk.
> *5:12–13).*

Now leprosy was a strange disease. Since the time of
Moses, no Jew had ever been cured of leprosy. There was
no cure known by doctors or religious leaders. In fact,
according to tradition, only *one* person could ever heal
this disease – the Messiah who was to come, the anointed one, the Christ.

He had hit a nerve and the reaction was yet to come.
What Jesus was doing was throwing down the gauntlet
to the religious authorities. He was saying this:

> *'Hey, you don't want to believe in me, but you're going to have
> to now. I've just done something that no mere man could ever
> do. I've performed a miracle that you say only the Messiah
> could do. So what does that make me?'*

Yet although there was no known cure, the book of
Leviticus (Lev. 13 – 14) gave lots of details of what to do
if someone was healed of leprosy. It was as if Moses

knew that one day, in the future, one would come who would be able to cure this disease. But, then again, didn't he prophesy 'the Prophet who was to come'? So he knew what he was doing.

> *'Then Jesus ordered him, "Don't tell anyone, but go, show yourself to the priest and offer the sacrifices that Moses commanded for your cleansing, as a testimony to them"' (Lk. 5:14).*

This is what Leviticus tells us. If someone *claimed* to be healed of leprosy, he had to go to the priests and offer a sacrifice of two birds and start a seven-day investigation to answer three questions. Did the person really have leprosy? Was he actually cured of leprosy? How did he get cured? Then, on the eighth day, a whole series of sacrifices would be offered.

So the cured individual was sent to the priests, as a *testimony* of what had just happened, and the only possible conclusion they could draw in this case was that Jesus *had* to be the Messiah.

> *'Yet the news about him spread all the more, so that crowds of people came to hear him and to be healed of their sicknesses' (Lk. 5:15).*

So the cat was out of the bag. Not only were the priests alerted to him, but news of this miracle spread throughout the land. A marker had been laid down. Follow that! And he did . . .

In healing the man of leprosy, he had proclaimed freedom for the prisoner and performed a miracle that only the Messiah could perform. Now he was going to *release the oppressed*. He was going to attempt the really impossible.

> *'Then they brought him a demon-possessed man who was blind and mute, and Jesus healed him, so that he could both talk and see' (Mt. 12:22).*

What was particularly special about this was that this man could not be healed by traditional exorcism. The Jewish practice required the rabbi to ask the demon its name and then order it to leave the person. Jesus himself employed this method in Luke 8:30:

> *'Jesus asked him, "What is your name?" "Legion," he replied, because many demons had gone into him.'*

But this man was mute, so no one could ask the demon's name. The rabbis would have been flummoxed. Not so Jesus, who healed him anyway. When he did so he again revealed his true identity and the authority of the Messiah, for this, too, was considered a miracle that only the Messiah could perform. The reaction of the crowd was interesting:

> *'All the people were astonished and said, "Could this be the Son of David?"' (Mt. 12:23).*

Could this be the Son of David? The people were now wondering out loud. They understood the significance of what they had witnessed, and 'Son of David' was a popular name for the Messiah.

So Jesus had proclaimed freedom for the prisoner and released the oppressed. Now he was going to *recover the sight of the blind*. But, again, this was to be no ordinary healing.

> *'As he went along, he saw a man blind from birth. His disciples asked him, "Rabbi, who sinned, this man or his parents,*

that he was born blind?" "Neither this man nor his parents
sinned," said Jesus, "but this happened so that the work of God
might be displayed in his life"' (Jn. 9:1–3).

This man had lived his whole life under a cloud, a life of
accusation as well as sightlessness. But his affliction was
to be used mightily by God, as the third verse showed.
Jesus healed him with some spit and mud, and on a
Sabbath no less. The Pharisees were mightily disturbed,
and interrogated both the man and his parents. The parents were cagey because they understood the significance of this healing:

'"We know he is our son," the parents answered, "and we
know he was born blind. But how he can see now, or who
opened his eyes, we don't know. Ask him. He is of age; he will
speak for himself." His parents said this because they were
afraid of the Jews, for already the Jews had decided that anyone
who acknowledged that Jesus was the Christ would be put out
of the synagogue' (Jn. 9:20–22).

The parents knew that this too was a miracle that only
the Messiah, the Christ, could perform, but they would
not say so, for fear of being excluded from the synagogue.

'Nobody has ever heard of opening the eyes of a man born
blind. If this man were not from God, he could do nothing' (Jn.
9:32–33).

There was no doubt that Jesus, through this and the
other two miracles, had boldly declared his
Messiahship. He said as much to John the Baptist's disciples, when they asked him whether he was the
Messiah:

> *'Jesus replied, "Go back and report to John what you hear and see: The blind receive sight, the lame walk, those who have leprosy are cured, the deaf hear, the dead are raised, and the good news is preached to the poor. Blessed is the man who does not fall away on account of me"' (Mt. 11:4–6).*

There's an interesting comment near the end of the Gospel of John, often overlooked:

> *'Jesus did many other miraculous signs in the presence of his disciples, which are not recorded in this book' (Jn. 20:30).*

We tend to think that what we read in the Gospels is all Jesus said and did. Far from it. John himself declares at the end of his Gospel that there is so much more he could have written, the world would not be large enough to hold all the words! That would have been counter-productive. It was important that he should get the point across in the most succinct and compact way. He must have been anticipating the low attention spans of us folk, two thousand years down the line! The Gospel gives us a snapshot, a verbal picture album of the highlights (and lowlights) of Jesus' life. And how did John manage to shoehorn all that potential material into his slim volume? In the next verse he explains:

> *'But these are written that you may believe that Jesus is the Christ, the Son of God, and that by believing you may have life in his name.'*

So the miraculous signs that John wrote about were there for a reason. Every one of them had a purpose; they weren't your common-or-garden miracles. They were Messianic miracles, signs pointing to Jesus as Messiah, as Christ. And special miracles they were, as we shall see.

There were, in fact, seven of them. First up is the water into wine at Cana. It was performed for his mother and all his disciples. As John said, this first miraculous sign was to reveal his glory to them and provide an anchor for their faith in him.

Interestingly, his second miraculous sign was also at Cana. This was the healing of the official's son, performed over a distance of around ten miles without Jesus even meeting the patient. As this was unheard of, it too was considered a miraculous sign of his Messiahship and resulted in the official and his whole household believing in Jesus and his claims.

Next was the healing at the Pool of Bethesda, performed on a Sabbath. This blatant disregard of tradition led to the first murmurings of murder by the religious Jewish establishment in Jerusalem.

Then there was the feeding of the five thousand, reported also in the other Gospels. If you think about it, this was remarkable in the extreme. We have heard this story so many times, seen it in so many movies, that its very familiarity lessens its impact. Yet a handful of loaves and fishes feeding the equivalent of a small football crowd? Food appearing from nowhere? This could be no conjuring trick; it was an act of creation par excellence. Surely only God Himself could create living creatures, even if the fish hardly had much of a meaningful experience, popping into the world only to pop down the throats of hungry people! And the idea that the whole baking process could be reproduced in a moment surely boggles the mind. The effect of this miraculous sign was significant. The people really took notice and were ready to proclaim Jesus the Messiah they had been awaiting so long, the conquering king. No wonder Jesus fled to the mountains before this could happen.

The fifth miraculous sign came later that day. It has provided fodder for comedians and has been scoffed at by liberals and sceptics, but the fact remains that Jesus actually walked three-and-a-half miles across the choppy waters of the Sea of Galilee. He wasn't drifting on ice, as a professor from Florida has suggested, neither did he wear invisible skis pulled along by an invisible motorboat. The fact that the phrase 'walking on water' has entered our vocabulary to signify an impossible task just shows it for what it was – an impossible task. But not for the Messiah – and in Matthew's account, the disciple Simon Peter, once he had cleared his lungs of the water he had almost drowned in after his attempt at water-walking, blurted out, '*Truly, you are the Son of God.*'

The sixth miraculous sign, the healing of the man born blind, has already been covered. The final one was probably the most dramatic of all. Although there have been accounts, even at the time of Jesus, of the dead being restored to life, there was none like the raising of Lazarus. Jesus could have restored his life at any time, but he chose to wait until the last possible moment, the fourth day, the point at which, according to Jewish tradition, the soul finally leaves the vicinity of the body and drifts away. Jesus wanted to do not just the improbable but, like walking on water, the impossible. Even the religious authorities acknowledged that this was a miraculous sign, and this particular miracle was the beginning of the end of Jesus' life and ministry on earth.

But they still didn't get it!

The Jews who had witnessed Jesus, seen the miracles and heard his proclamations still didn't really get it until afterwards. This is why, after his resurrection, Jesus had to explain the whole thing to the men he encountered on the road to Emmaus:

> 'He said to them, "How foolish you are, and how slow of heart
> to believe all that the prophets have spoken!" . . . And begin-
> ning with Moses and all the Prophets, he explained to them
> what was said in all the Scriptures concerning himself' (Lk.
> 24:25,27).

And to the rest of the disciples later that day:

> 'He said to them, "This is what I told you while I was still with
> you: Everything must be fulfilled that is written about me in
> the Law of Moses, the Prophets and the Psalms." Then he
> opened their minds so they could understand the Scriptures'
> (Lk. 24:44–45).

If the disciples, who had lived with him and witnessed
the events of his remarkable life, needed such an explanation, you can be sure that there was a general ignorance
of his mission during his lifetime. It was as if the director
of a particularly confusing movie had to appear on screen
at the end to explain the plot to a mystified audience.

Evidence of this abounds. For example, on Palm
Sunday, after Jesus appeared outside Jerusalem riding
on a donkey to fulfil the Messianic prophecy in
Zechariah 9:9, his disciples' reaction was striking:

> 'At first his disciples did not understand all this. Only after
> Jesus was glorified did they realise that these things had been
> written about him and that they had done these things to him'
> (Jn. 12:16).

There is further evidence of how wrong they were in
their expectations on Palm Sunday:

> 'Many people spread their cloaks on the road, while others
> spread branches they had cut in the fields. Those who went

ahead and those who followed shouted, "Hosanna!" "Blessed
is he who comes in the name of the Lord!" "Blessed is the com-
ing kingdom of our father David!" "Hosanna in the highest!"'
(Mk. 11:8–10).

If this passage were shown to a present-day religious
Jew, one question would be on his lips. '*This happened in*
Passover season? Are you sure?' This curious reaction is
because so much about this episode screams 'Feast of
Tabernacles', the feast of Israel that wasn't to occur for
another six months or so.

First, the words spoken. They are from Psalm 118, one
of the great psalms looking forwards to the Messiah:

> '*Blessed is he who comes in the name of the* LORD' *(Ps. 118:26).*

Secondly, their actions. They spread branches before
him. From a combined reading of all Gospel accounts, it
is notable that the very branches themselves echoed
what happened at the Feast of Tabernacles.

So why would they do this? Because the Feast of
Tabernacles was the feast most associated with the com-
ing of the Messiah. There is a clear reference to this in
Zechariah:

> '*Then the survivors from all the nations that have attacked*
> *Jerusalem will go up year after year to worship the King, the*
> LORD *Almighty, and to celebrate the Feast of Tabernacles. If*
> *any of the peoples of the earth do not go up to Jerusalem to*
> *worship the King, the* LORD *Almighty, they will have no rain'*
> *(Zech. 14:16–17).*

This was the Messiah they were expecting, the one who
would rule the nations from Jerusalem. This is why they
were laying the branches and chanting the Messianic

psalm. They thought that this time had come, albeit six months too early! Their king had come, or so they thought. A few days later Jesus was dead, and many fell away as a result of their mistaken expectations. Yet between Palm Sunday and the Crucifixion, Jesus had spoken very publicly about this, declaring to the Jewish religious establishment:

> *'For I tell you, you will not see me again until you say, "Blessed is he who comes in the name of the Lord"' (Mt. 23:39).*

This is the very same Messianic psalm chanted on Palm Sunday, so they were fully aware of its significance. He was telling them, most clearly and unambiguously, the following: *'I'll be back!'*

We have the benefit of hindsight (and two thousand years of scholarship); the Jews living at the time of Jesus had just their five senses. So they didn't really get it until afterwards. It doesn't mean that they were particularly thick or ignorant; in fact their knowledge of their own scriptures would put us to shame. They had the knowledge, just not the application. Jesus came as a most unexpected Messiah, and so fixed were their ideas as to how the Messiah should have acted that further explanations were needed.

6

Rabbi

*Question: What was so special about Jesus' teaching
methods?*

It is surely ironic that the people who could best understand the teachings of Jesus were not Bible scholars,
New Testament theologians or Divinity professors but
the first-century Jews who were there to hear them at
first hand – but who basically didn't get it! It wasn't just
that Jesus spoke their language and they were witnesses
to these teachings, it was that every nuance, word play
and saying was steeped in the culture of the day. It was
as if a thirty-first-century Esperanto-speaking historian
were studying the works of Bob Marley, thinking that all
they needed was a library of references on twentieth-
century Jamaican patois and a good training in historical
analysis, but ultimately failing without the benefits of
ganja, reggae and the laid-back Caribbean lifestyle. You
just had to be there to get it.

So Jesus was a rabbi. He was addressed as such by a
lawyer, a rich man, Pharisees, Sadducees and ordinary
Jews, so you can take it as read. The word comes from the
Hebrew word *rav* and its original meaning was 'master',

though by Jesus' day it was also used as a title for a teacher (though it wasn't until after AD 70 that it was used formally in this way). His ministry was typical of those times: fully itinerant, never in one place for long.

To fully appreciate the teachings of a first-century Jewish rabbi, one really needs to get into the skin of a first-century Jew, or at least do so by proxy. So, in this chapter we are all first-century Jews. We are going to sample some of Jesus' teachings through first-century Jewish eyes, rather than through western interpretations of English translations of Greek scripture written by Jews who would be thinking the words in Hebrew or Aramaic. These will be familiar stories, but will seem new to you because you will hear them through a Hebraic filter. Hold on to your yarmulkes, we're going on a journey.

There you were, minding your own business, among the throng at the gates of the temple, joining the longer of the two queues leading to the livestock enclosures. You were there to pay your annual temple dues and buy your Passover sacrifice, in your case a dove on account of your lowly station in life. Hours later, you could see, hear and smell the object of your visit and were just fiddling around in your pouch for the half-shekel when a loud voice bellowed from behind you. An angry, insistent voice, growing louder by the second as it approached. You couldn't turn round: your transaction had begun. But the loud crash forced a reaction and you twisted your head to see the commotion by the stalls of the money changers. The carefully arranged stacks of coins were no more; money was strewn over the straw, rolling in the dust, as the benches lay on their side, flanked by red-faced angry men. But none was angrier than the one who was at the heart of the mayhem and he was now striding towards you . . .

'Is it not written,' he declared in a firm, controlled voice, as he made steady progress across the temple court, *'"My house will be called a house of prayer for all nations"?'* (Mk. 11:17).

Time froze. You may have been only a poor Jew, but you knew your scriptures. Everyone had some knowledge of the prophets and wise ones, and the words spoken by this Jesus, the rabbi from Nazareth, were very familiar. They had been spoken by the prophet Isaiah hundreds of years earlier, words that described how things should be in God's house. Uncomfortable words, because everyone knew how things were, that they were not how they ought to be. Trying times, but all too easy to blame it on the Romans, cursed be their name. As if he was reading your thoughts, his next words drove home like a stake to the heart. As Jesus spoke them, he raised his arms, as if to encircle everyone who was there, and slowly rotated them in a sweeping motion.

'But you have made it "a den of robbers".'

Suddenly there was an even louder commotion, a cacophony of voices: not the coarse speech of the traders but the cultured whines of the learned, the priests themselves, as well as some Pharisees. The words had had a particular impact on them, because they were the intended targets. And how clever of the rabbi.

He was reminding everyone of a most shameful episode in Jewish history, and it was the prophet Jeremiah who expressed it the most clearly. The prophet had stood in this very same place all those hundreds of years ago. He had read out a list of sins of the people, but had also told them that only if they changed their ways would they be saved and allowed to live in the land. He was not a happy man, and he accused the people of his day of hypocrisy and turning the temple into a 'den of robbers'.

> 'Has this house, which bears my Name, become a den of robbers to you? But I have been watching! declares the LORD' (Jer. 7:11).

But there was more than that, and it was what Jeremiah said next that resonated so strongly with the priests who were smarting under Jesus' onslaught: 'Remember Shiloh!'

This meant something to the Jews of Jesus' day as well as those of Jeremiah's day. It was a warning.

These days, if we want to give a warning we can say something like *remember Hiroshima* or *remember Vietnam* or *remember Bill Clinton*. These words trigger an image that serves as a warning to a group of people who do remember these things. So, what did *Shiloh* conjure up?

Imagine you are an eye-witness. The next words spoken by Jeremiah would come to mind:

> 'Go now to the place in Shiloh where I first made a dwelling for my Name, and see what I did to it because of the wickedness of my people Israel. While you were doing all these things, declares the LORD, I spoke to you again and again, but you did not listen; I called you, but you did not answer. Therefore, what I did to Shiloh I will now do to the house that bears my Name, the temple you trust in, the place I gave to you and your fathers. I will thrust you from my presence, just as I did all your brothers, the people of Ephraim' (Jer. 7:12–14).

And you remember what happened at Shiloh. You are taken back further, to the days of the prophet Samuel, the days of the Judges of Israel.

It was at Shiloh that the Israelites lost the Ark of the Lord's covenant, their holiest possession, to the

Philistines. Led by a corrupt priesthood, they used this sacred object as a talisman, thinking that it would gain them victory in war. Instead they were massively defeated and thirty thousand men were killed. It was a national disaster, commemorated by the name given to the grandson of Eli the priest – *Ichabod*, meaning 'The glory has departed' (from Israel).

So you stood there, witnessing the confrontation between Jesus and the priests. In that single condemnation, all who were there would have no doubt that Jesus was declaring judgement on the current corrupt priesthood, which had allowed the sacred temple to be profaned by moneychangers and traders, and implying that God would put an end to this temple and priesthood, just as He had done all those years ago at Shiloh.

The anger of the priests and the Pharisees was palpable, and although you did not know it at the time, they would now begin to plot to kill Jesus. It wasn't just because their pride was hurt by the condemnations from this 'upstart rabbi', but because they could sense something else . . .

'The whole crowd was amazed at his teaching' (Mk. 11:18).

You weren't the only one who marvelled at how this Jesus could strike at the heart of the situation with a single declaration. You looked around at the murmurings. You could sense the fear of the priests, but also the utmost awe of the pilgrims and worshippers. This man spoke to the heart: he expressed what others could only vaguely imagine, with words spoken in boldness. *They won't take this lying down*, you sensed, as the priests milled together in shared annoyance.

One single phrase: *'My house will be called a house of prayer for all nations. But you have made it a den of robbers.'*

Yet the mind of the listener was able to make the connections. They would first have understood the true purpose of the temple, from the words of the prophet Isaiah. They would also have been familiar with Jeremiah's condemnation of how low things had sunk. Then they would have understood the warning that the ultimate fate of the temple and the priesthood would be as it had been at the time of Samuel, with the loss of the Ark at Shiloh.

This was how it was, it wasn't an illusion. Rather, it was all an *allusion*, a teaching style used by Jesus, along with other rabbis of his day. Working on the premise that the hearers were thoroughly familiar with key scriptures, it used connections between different scriptures to make a point. A modern-day allusion would make use of media sound-bites that are as familiar to us as the Old Testament scriptures were to a first-century Jew.

'We were told "no whitewash", but we ended up with Iraq-gate.'

Anyone with an interest in political history would immediately understand this. The 'whitewash' quote is an allusion to the 'no whitewash at the White House' declaration by President Nixon just before his lies caught him out in the Watergate scandal. The reference to 'Iraq-gate' makes the statement into a double allusion: the use of the word '-gate' creates a link in people's minds between the Iraq situation and Watergate, thereby implying the more recent events are as politically scandalous as the original ones.

Jesus also used allusion when he first dropped this particular bombshell:

> 'The Son of Man must suffer many things and be rejected by the elders, chief priests and teachers of the law, and he must be killed and on the third day be raised to life' (Lk. 9:22).

This declaration, his first to the disciples concerning his impending death and resurrection, is packed with references to familiar scriptures, but perhaps the allusion least familiar to us is his reference to his resurrection on the *third* day. Apart from the obvious connection to the three days of Jonah in the belly of the fish, the scripture to which this actually alludes is Hosea 6:2:

> '*After two days he will revive us; on the third day he will restore us, that we may live in his presence.*'

This scripture has been a key one in the Jewish hope for resurrection at the end of the age. By using it in the context of his own future, Jesus offers, to all who hear and understand, this hope for their own lives too.

Jesus was no ordinary teacher, or rabbi. He spoke with confidence and with an authority that amazed some and antagonized others. Yet a lot of his teaching, in its original context and sense, has been lost to us. This is not our fault, neither is it the fault of those who teach us. It is simply a consequence of history, the sad fact of a decision made by the Christian church in its formative years. It was the loosening of the bonds that tied it to its roots, the felling of the great olive tree of Romans 9 – 11. Outwardly this manifested itself in the horrific persecutions of the Jews, but inwardly the church suffocated itself by removing all traces of the Hebraic origins of its faith. It was not quite self-destruction, but the church denied itself so many blessings. Just as a smoker feeds toxins into his system to feed his destructive habit, so the Gentile Christian church had taken on pagan worldviews that ultimately were not going to do it any favours at all.

It could have been so different. To give you a flavour of what has been lost, we will look at some of the

Sermon on the Mount in Matthew 5 – 7 and see how first-century Jews would have understood the words.

> *'Do not think that I have come to abolish the Law or the Prophets; I have not come to abolish them but to fulfil them'* (Mt. 5:17).

Interestingly, this verse is the only saying of Jesus that appears in the Talmud, though with extreme penalties attached. The Talmud says, *'The one who destroys even the smallest letter of the Law, the sin is so great, that if it could be done, the whole world would be destroyed.'* To abolish the Torah is a concept of total horror to the religious Jewish mind, but to fulfil it is to interpret it properly. This is exactly what Jesus had in mind:

> *'I tell you the truth, until heaven and earth disappear, not the smallest letter, not the least stroke of a pen, will by any means disappear from the Law until everything is accomplished'* (Mt. 5:18).

Why the translators couldn't just state the actual words used, tickles me. Some translations use the words 'jot' and 'tittle' for what is described here as 'the smallest letter' and 'the least stroke of a pen'. Why not call a spade a spade and tell it how it is – the 'jot' is in fact the Hebrew letter, 'yod'. And yes, it *is* the smallest letter in the Hebrew alphabet. The Talmud says, *'If all the world gathered to destroy the yod, the smallest letter in the Law, they would not succeed.'*[1] The 'tittle' is the part of the Hebrew letter that distinguishes certain letters that look alike, so I suppose 'the least stroke of the pen' describes it well.

> *'But I tell you that anyone who is angry with his brother will be subject to judgment. Again, anyone who says to his*

> *brother, "Raca," is answerable to the Sanhedrin. But anyone*
> *who says, "You fool!" will be in danger of the fire of hell' (Mt.*
> *5:22).*

This word 'Raca' means 'empty-headed' or incompetent and its use was a serious matter indeed in those days, which explains the extreme reaction. We find more enlightenment when we read what it says in the Talmud. Baba Mezia 58b declares that everyone who descends into hell will eventually be released, except for adulterers and those who shame neighbours in public. Baba Mezia 59b goes further by stating that a man would be better off jumping into a furnace than shaming a neighbour.

> *'Therefore, if you are offering your gift at the altar and there*
> *remember that your brother has something against you, leave*
> *your gift there in front of the altar. First go and be reconciled*
> *to your brother; then come and offer your gift' (Mt. 5:23–24).*

As with the previous passage, this is all about the way believers dealt with each other, rather than their relationship with God. The Mishnah says, *'The transgressions a man commits against God on the Day of Atonement are atoned, but the one against his neighbour is only atoned when his neighbour is satisfied.'*[2] If you don't get it right with your fellow man, God is just not interested.

> *'You have heard that it was said, "Do not commit adultery."*
> *But I tell you that anyone who looks at a woman lustfully has*
> *already committed adultery with her in his heart' (Mt.*
> *5:27–28).*

This saying uses a rabbinic technique known as *kal vachomer*, meaning 'light and heavy'. What this means is that if a minor thing is true, then so is a major one, but more so; or if something 'light' is true (e.g. owing someone £100 is a problem), then something 'heavy' is also true (e.g. owing £200 is a bigger problem). So, if lusting after someone ('light') is a sin, how much more sinful would be the actual act of adultery ('heavy').

Jesus uses *kal vachomer* a lot, and nowhere does it need to be understood more than in the following verses:

> *'If your right eye causes you to sin, gouge it out and throw it away. It is better for you to lose one part of your body than for your whole body to be thrown into hell. And if your right hand causes you to sin, cut it off and throw it away. It is better for you to lose one part of your body than for your whole body to go into hell' (Mt. 5:29–30).*

The essence is that if a sin can be nipped in the bud while it is still in its 'light' stage (just your right hand), you can be protected from the implications of the 'heavy' stage (going to hell). It is important to see these verses as a figurative example, rather than taking them literally, otherwise there would be a lot of Captain Hooks in heaven!

> *'Be careful not to do your "acts of righteousness" before men, to be seen by them. If you do, you will have no reward from your Father in heaven. So when you give to the needy, do not announce it with trumpets, as the hypocrites do in the synagogues and on the streets, to be honoured by men. I tell you the truth, they have received their reward in full. But when you give to the needy, do not let your left hand know what your right hand is doing, so that your giving may be in secret. Then your Father, who sees what is done in secret, will reward you' (Mt. 6:1–4).*

The behaviour of the religious Jews at the time of Jesus is by no means typical. The Talmud states that Rabbi Eleazor taught, '*He who gives his charity in secret is even greater than Moses our teacher.*'[3] It also tells us that Rabbi Chana used to secretly leave grain outside his door at night so that the poor could hide their shame in the darkness.[4] There's an interesting background to the use of trumpets in this passage. In the Women's Court of the temple during the first century there were thirteen trumpet-shaped collection boxes for alms, which made a specific sound as the coins entered. These containers were wide at the bottom and narrow at the top, resembling a trumpet. Often the Pharisees who wished to boast would drop a large number of coins in at one time, which was called 'sounding the trumpet'. It was this practice of letting everyone know how much they were giving that Jesus was speaking against.

> '*And when you pray, do not be like the hypocrites, for they love to pray standing in the synagogues and on the street corners to be seen by men. I tell you the truth, they have received their reward in full. But when you pray, go into your room, close the door and pray to your Father, who is unseen. Then your Father, who sees what is done in secret, will reward you. And when you pray, do not keep on babbling like pagans, for they think they will be heard because of their many words*' (Mt. 6:5–7).

In the Talmud, Rabbi Eleazor taught that anyone whose prayers were just routine or who considered praying itself as a bit of a bother was not genuinely praying at all.[5] As an example of the ostentatious manner of some religious Jews, the Talmud tells us of Rabbi Akiva, who was so frantic in his bowings and prostrations that the whole process would take him from one corner of the synagogue to the other![6]

> *'For yours is the kingdom and the power and the glory for ever.*
> *Amen' (Mt. 6:13).*

The Mishnah notes that the response to the high priest pronouncing the Divine Name was *'Blessed be the name of the glory of his kingdom for ever and ever.'*[7] Apparently this response was delivered in a whisper, but later *'they ordered that men should say it in a loud voice, because of the carping of the heretics'*, a reference to those Jews who followed Jesus and were not afraid to admit as much during the synagogue service![8]

> *'When you fast, do not look sombre as the hypocrites do, for they disfigure their faces to show men they are fasting. I tell you the truth, they have received their reward in full. But when you fast, put oil on your head and wash your face, so that it will not be obvious to men that you are fasting, but only to your Father, who is unseen; and your Father, who sees what is done in secret, will reward you' (Mt. 6:16–18).*

This disfiguring of their faces was done with ashes, and the act of fasting is described in the Mishnah.[9] First, you stopped work, then no eating, drinking, sex, washing or bathing, though you could eat at night. At the time of Jesus, Jews were expected to fast at least on the second and fifth days of the week.

> *'The eye is the lamp of the body. If your eyes are good, your whole body will be full of light. But if your eyes are bad, your whole body will be full of darkness' (Mt. 6:22–23).*

Any Jew listening to this would have known it was absolutely nothing to do with light and darkness. It was a popular saying at the time, that if someone had a 'good eye' they were generous; if they had a 'bad eye' they were mean-spirited. The Mishnah says, '*The person with a good eye gave the 40th part of the first fruit of the heave offering for the maintaining of the priests, while the person with the evil eye gave only a 60th.*'[10] It also says that '*he that gives, but wants a monopoly on giving and does not want others to be able to give too, is considered to have an evil eye.*'[11]

Generosity is a good thing and a positive influence on your well-being: the result is that your body 'will be full of light'. This makes sense of the next verse, which otherwise might seem a bit detached and 'off the point':

> '*No-one can serve two masters. Either he will hate the one and love the other, or he will be devoted to the one and despise the other. You cannot serve both God and Money*' (Mt. 6:24).

So Jesus is talking about how we use our personal finances, not our eyesight.

> '*Do not judge, or you too will be judged. For in the same way as you judge others, you will be judged, and with the measure you use, it will be measured to you*' (Mt. 7:1–2).

Not everything that Jesus taught was new and unique; much of it was simply his take on a rabbinical saying of the time. This is a good example. The Talmud says, '*Rabbi Hillel said, "Judge not your neighbour until you have come into his place."*'[12] Elsewhere in the Talmud it says, '*Whatever measure a man metes, it shall be measured to him again.*'[13] And Rabbi Meier said, '*The measure by which one measures will be measured out to him,*'[14] The Talmud states, '*All the measures have ceased, except the rule "measure for measure" has not ceased.*'[15] To follow this theme into familiar territory, how about this one: '*Rabbi Yochanan bar Kokba said, "Do they say, 'Take the splinter out of your own eye'? We are taught to remove the beam from your own eye."*'[16]

In another rabbinic statement, Rabbi Tarfon said, *'I wonder if there is anyone in this generation that accepts reproof? For when one says, "Remove the mote from your eye," he would answer, "Remove the beam that is in between your eyes."'*

> *'So in everything, do to others what you would have them do to you, for this sums up the Law and the Prophets'* (Mt. 7:12).

There's a fairly well-known story that illustrates this principle. It is recorded in the Talmud and speaks of Rabbi Hillel, a contemporary of Jesus:[17]

> *'Once a pagan approached Shammai and said to him, "I will become a convert, but only if you can teach me the entire Torah while I am standing on one foot." Shammai drove him away with a yardstick which he was holding. Then the pagan put the same request to Hillel, and Hillel answered him, "Do not do to anyone else what is hateful to you. This is the entire Torah. All the rest is only a commentary about it. Now go and learn."'*

To finish the chapter, here are a few more short passages for your delectation:

> *'On the last and greatest day of the Feast, Jesus stood and said in a loud voice, "If anyone is thirsty, let him come to me and drink"'* (Jn. 7:37).

This was the Feast of Tabernacles, or *Succot*. According to the Talmud, a golden jar would be filled with water from the Pool of Siloam and the water would be poured out with great rejoicing and entertainment over several days.[18] It was said that anyone who had never watched the festival at this time, the time of Water-Drawing, had never seen joy in their life.

> *'When Jesus spoke again to the people, he said, "I am the light of the world. Whoever follows me will never walk in darkness, but will have the light of life"' (Jn. 8:12).*

These words were spoken at the end of Succot, when it was the custom, according to the Talmud, to light four great menorahs (lampstands) in the outer court of the temple.[19] It was said that there was no house in Jerusalem that did not reflect the light of these menorahs, and that the light was so great that women at home could sort out grains of wheat by it.[20] Against this backdrop, picture the scene: Jesus standing in the temple area, surrounded by this majestic shimmering glow, speaking those life-affirming words. Incredible.

> *'In reply Jesus said: "A man was going down from Jerusalem to Jericho, when he fell into the hands of robbers. They stripped him of his clothes, beat him and went away, leaving him half-dead. A priest happened to be going down the same road, and when he saw the man, he passed by on the other side. So too, a Levite, when he came to the place and saw him, passed by on the other side"' (Lk. 10:30–32).*

The actions of the priest and Levite were consistent with their training, as contact with a dead body would make them ritually unclean. They weren't even allowed to visit cemeteries, just in case they stepped on a grave. The Talmud states that a body found lying in a road should be moved out of the way, to protect the purity of any passing priest.[21] Of course the actions of the priest and Levite may have been correct in terms of the 'letter of the Law', but the spirit of the Law would surely have included compassion for the stricken man.

This is just a small collection of examples of Jesus' teaching methods. If you want to go further into this, there are books listed in Appendix B that will help you to do so.

Notes

(All the following are references to the Talmud)

[1] Devarim Rabba 5:11.
[2] Mishnah Yoma 8:9.
[3] Baba Bathra 9b.
[4] Berakoth 58b.
[5] Berakoth 29b.
[6] Berakoth 31a.
[7] Mishnah Yoma 6:2.
[8] Pesahim 56a.
[9] Taamid 1:6.
[10] Mishnah Terumoth 4:3.
[11] Avot 5:15.
[12] Mishnah Avot 2:4.
[13] Mishnah Sotah 1:7.
[14] Babylonian Sanhedrin 100a.
[15] Bereshith Raba 9:13.
[16] Babylonian Baba Bathra 176b.
[17] Shabbath 31a.
[18] Mishnah Sukkah 4:9, 5:1.
[19] Mishnah Sukkah 5:2–4.
[20] Sukkah 53a.
[21] Erubin 17b.

7

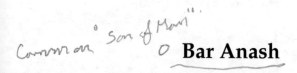

Common on "Son of Man"

Bar Anash

Question: What title did Jesus most often use for himself and why?

When it came to using names for himself, there's one that Jesus preferred above all: *Son of Man*. Every time you see this expression in the Gospels, it is Jesus himself speaking. It was important to him, and it must therefore be important for us to find out why.

Why he chose this name has occupied the brains of Bible scholars for centuries, but let's first consider the reactions of those he moved among in Judea and Galilee. After all, the Gospels tell us the words Jesus used with those he met, whether simple fishermen, Pharisees or the chief priest. It's them he is speaking to, not stuffy old academics and theologians living hundreds of years later in strange lands over the sea. So, you're a first-century Jew, and a miracle-working rabbi is calling himself 'Son of Man'. How would you react to this? What would it have meant to you?

In the Hebrew scriptures, this expression appears in three places. First, mainly in the Psalms, there is a poetic use that contrasts us lowly men with the majesty and greatness of God Himself.

> '*O* LORD, *what is man that you care for him, the son of man that you think of him?*' *(Ps. 144:3).*

Secondly, it's a personal term of endearment used by God in His dealings with the prophet Ezekiel, throughout the book of his name.

> '*He said to me, "Son of man, stand up on your feet and I will speak to you"*' *(Ezek. 2:1).*

Thirdly, and most significantly, it's a term used in the book of Daniel, one of the few verses written in the Aramaic language rather than the Hebrew of the rest of the Bible. The Aramaic term is *bar anash*.

> '*In my vision at night I looked, and there before me was one like a son of man, coming with the clouds of heaven. He approached the Ancient of Days and was led into his presence. He was given authority, glory and sovereign power; all peoples, nations and men of every language worshipped him. His dominion is an everlasting dominion that will not pass away, and his kingdom is one that will never be destroyed*' *(Dan. 7:13–14).*

This passage identifies a majestic supernatural being, coming in the clouds and receiving authority from God, the Ancient of Days, and then, incredibly, it describes him as being *like* a 'son of man'. In other words, this apparently divine person seems to be just like you and me, a human being, a 'son of man'. A man, yet *more* than a man.

This single passage has been said to be the clearest announcement of the Redeemer ever developed by ancient Judaism. In which case, what better scripture to identify with if you are that very Redeemer!

So that is what Jesus did.

Jesus is recorded as calling himself 'Son of Man' around fifty times, allowing for duplications in Matthew, Mark and Luke. Of those utterances, around 20 per cent emphasize his humanity, his identification with the human race, in the sense that we are all 'sons of men'. Of course the issue that plagued the Church Fathers concerning the humanity of Jesus was irrelevant to the people who met him, spoke to him and ate with him in first-century Judea and Galilee. He didn't need to remind them of his humanity, but his divinity was a different matter. And that is why 80 per cent of the times Jesus called himself 'Son of Man' it was in a supernatural sense, either describing his role as redeemer –

> *'For the Son of Man came to seek and to save what was lost'*
> *(Lk. 19:10).*

– or his future role, when he returns to earth:

> *'At that time the sign of the Son of Man will appear in the sky, and all the nations of the earth will mourn. They will see the Son of Man coming on the clouds of the sky, with power and great glory' (Mt. 24:30).*

Doesn't he also call himself the Son of God? That's a good question, because interestingly, in the whole of the Gospels, Jesus rarely mentions this term, and in the following situation he demonstrates his preferred name:

> *'I tell you the truth, whoever hears my word and believes him who sent me has eternal life and will not be condemned; he has crossed over from death to life. I tell you the truth, a time is coming and has now come when the dead will hear the voice of the Son of God and those who hear will live. For as the Father*

has life in himself, so he has granted the Son to have life in himself. And he has given him authority to judge because he is the Son of Man' (Jn. 5:24–27).

Amazingly, every other mention of 'Son of God' is by a whole cast of characters, a true cross-section of Gospel personages, including Satan and his demons, Jesus' disciples, the high priest, a Roman centurion, an angel, John the Baptist, Martha and the Gospel writers themselves. But not Jesus himself: he always preferred 'Son of Man'.

The reason, again, was Jesus' very real need to authenticate his ministry by identifying with a concept already familiar to those around him. 'Son of Man' was a familiar concept to his Jewish listeners. 'Son of God' would have meant nothing to them theologically, as it appears nowhere in the Old Testament.

That said, there are twenty-two mentions of the Son of God in the Gospels, by the people already mentioned. Where did they get this concept from? Plucked it out of the air? Well, eight mentions are by angels or demons, who would have had special knowledge 'from the horse's mouth', so to speak. Three mentions are by the Gospel writers, writing many years after the event and familiar with the concept by then.

That leaves eleven declarations to account for. What is clear is that whenever Jesus was declared directly the Son of God, he never actually denied it, so he certainly identified with it.

In Matthew 26:63, the high priest proclaimed, *'Tell us if you are the Christ, the Son of God.'* This is how Jesus answered:

> *'Yes, it is as you say,' Jesus replied. 'But I say to all of you: In the future you will see the Son of Man sitting at the right hand of the Mighty One and coming on the clouds of heaven.'*

So he didn't deny it; he merely corrected their phraseology. Similarly with Nathanael, who, full of faith, declared, *'Rabbi, you are the Son of God; you are the King of Israel'* (Jn. 1:49). Jesus responded:

> *' "You believe because I told you I saw you under the fig tree. You shall see greater things than that." He then added, "I tell you the truth, you shall see heaven open, and the angels of God ascending and descending on the Son of Man"' (Jn. 1:50–51).*

Again, no denial: just a correction. Jesus was merely intent on getting his message across through every means possible.

Even though we read of no instance where Jesus specifically declared himself the Son of God, we can see he was certainly identified with this concept from the sheer variety of people who called him by this name. In fact, humanly speaking, Jesus would have had every reason to keep schtum about its use, because this is what, ultimately, got him crucified! *Blasphemy! How dare he call himself God, or the Son of God or whatever? Hear O Israel, the Lord our God, the Lord is One.*

Perhaps this is why the demons were very vocal in their use of this term. They wanted him to get into trouble. Perhaps this is how people like Nathanael and Martha got to hear of the term. Perhaps Jesus was concerned that his earthly mission might be brought to a halt if his true divine nature was seized upon by the religious authorities prematurely. It matters not, because Jesus never denied being the Son of God and even went around actively proving that he was divine by his words and his actions.

Let us build up the case for the prosecution at Jesus' trial before the Sanhedrin. The high priest would surely need evidence for this declaration:

> *'I charge you under oath by the living God: Tell us if you are the Christ, the Son of God' (Mt. 26:63).*

He had to be sure of his position, because if Jesus had declared himself the Son of God it was blasphemy, punishable by death, in the eyes of the Jewish court.

There is evidence aplenty, far too much to mention here, so what you are going to get now is a whistle-stop tour. We start with some of Jesus' own declarations that he was the Son of Man. Interestingly it wasn't this name that militated against him, it was the context that sent out the signals. Let's see:

> *'"But so that you may know that the Son of Man has authority on earth to forgive sins.. .." Then he said to the paralytic, "Get up, take your mat and go home"' (Mt. 9:6).*

You only have to judge the reaction of the Pharisees to understand what Jesus was demonstrating here: his authority to forgive sins. He was acting as God.

> *'For the Son of Man is Lord of the Sabbath' (Mt. 12:8).*

The Sabbath was a divine institution, initiated in Creation week and ratified by the finger of God Himself on Mount Sinai. The Lord of the Sabbath could only be God Himself.

> *'For the Son of Man is going to come in his Father's glory with his angels, and then he will reward each person according to what he has done' (Mt. 16:27).*

A reference to God as his Father and his own role in the grand court of humanity at the end of days seems to seal the deal.

> *'Jesus said to them, "I tell you the truth, at the renewal of all things, when the Son of Man sits on his glorious throne, you who have followed me will also sit on twelve thrones, judging the twelve tribes of Israel"'* (Mt. 19:28).

Another reference to the grand court, with jobs for the boys also offered.

> *'At that time the sign of the Son of Man will appear in the sky, and all the nations of the earth will mourn. They will see the Son of Man coming on the clouds of the sky, with power and great glory'* (Mt. 24:30).

Outside comic books, no mere mortals have ever been seen coming in the clouds.

> *'No-one has ever gone into heaven except the one who came from heaven – the Son of Man'* (Jn. 3:13).

At that time heaven was a divine address; only a divine person would have appeared on the census forms.

Also, in the Gospel of John, there is the matter of Jesus' seven proclamations:

> *'I am the living bread that came down from heaven. If anyone eats of this bread, he will live for ever. This bread is my flesh, which I will give for the life of the world'* (Jn. 6:51).

> *'When Jesus spoke again to the people, he said, "I am the light of the world. Whoever follows me will never walk in darkness, but will have the light of life"'* (Jn. 8:12).

> *'I am the gate; whoever enters through me will be saved. He will come in and go out, and find pasture'* (Jn. 10:9).

'I am the good shepherd. The good shepherd lays down his life for the sheep' (Jn. 10:11).

'Jesus said to her, "I am the resurrection and the life. He who believes in me will live, even though he dies"' (Jn. 11:25).

'Jesus answered, "I am the way and the truth and the life. No-one comes to the Father except through me"' (Jn. 14:6).

'I am the true vine, and my Father is the gardener' (Jn. 15:1).

No prizes for the common factor here. It is Jesus introducing himself with the words, '*I am . . .*'

These two words alone were enough to declare his identity. To any listening Jew it was as if he were shouting from the rooftops, '*It is me, the Son of God.*' To understand this we need to return to the time of Moses, to his encounter with the burning bush in Exodus 3:13–14:

'Moses said to God, "Suppose I go to the Israelites and say to them, 'The God of your fathers has sent me to you,' and they ask me, 'What is his name?' Then what shall I tell them?" God said to Moses, "I AM WHO I AM. This is what you are to say to the Israelites: 'I AM has sent me to you.'"'

You've heard the expression that someone is too big for his boots: '*There goes the great I AM.*' Well, this is where it comes from. Like many of our popular expressions, it comes from the Bible. In this case, it is a solemn and awesome episode, the first time God really identifies Himself by name to His people.

The Hebrew word used here is *Ehyeh*, translated as 'I am', but more correctly as 'I will be'. It is the root of the divine name YHWH used throughout the Old Testament, incorrectly transliterated as Jehovah.

So Jesus identified with God in the most overt and provocative way he could. He was truly the great I am.

He said as much to a Jewish gathering:

> '"I tell you the truth," Jesus answered, "before Abraham was born, I AM!"' (Jn. 8:58).

And they tried to stone him for blasphemy.

He said as much to the chief priest at his trial:

> '"I am," said Jesus. "And you will see the Son of Man sitting at the right hand of the Mighty One and coming on the clouds of heaven"' (Mk. 14:62).

And the chief priest tore his clothes and declared him a blasphemer, worthy of death.

So Jesus was truly divine; he knew it and demonstrated it. But he didn't come down to this earth to boast of his credentials and gather a band of disciples; he had a very real mission to perform. There was a reason behind it all. He had come, as his name Jesus (Yeshua) indicated, *to save his people*. He had come to be their redeemer.

Jesus really needed to get his point across, in words as well as actions. He had three years to demonstrate exactly why he had come to earth. He had to show them what a redeemer is and what a redeemer does.

A redeemer is needed because of these few stark words in the Letter to the Hebrews:

> 'Without the shedding of blood there is no forgiveness' (Heb. 9:22).

The story leading up to this can be very long if you're new to the whole concept, but as you've already got so far, here it is in précis:

Adam and Eve had it made. They were tempted by Satan and they sinned. They fell, the world fell, and humankind was separated from God. There needed to be a way for humanity to undo all the bad stuff and get back to God. Animal sacrifices were instituted, but were always a temporary measure, sinking into a meaningless ritual. The real trouble is in the heart of man. Only a permanent solution will do, but blood needs to be shed, because that's how it works (not for us to argue). A redeemer is needed to bring this about – a substitute for the animal sacrifice. Jesus came to fulfil that role. As (mainly) Gentiles living in a later time, in a far-off land, in an alien culture, we need to gain an understanding of things that would have been instinctive to the Hebrew soul – not that they ever realized that privilege at the time!

So how did he go about it? Here is the Gospel, the Good News of Jesus, Son of God. You've heard it all before, but let's face it: we never tire of hearing it, do we?

> 'For God was pleased to have all his fullness dwell in him, and through him to reconcile to himself all things, whether things on earth or things in heaven, by making peace through his blood, shed on the cross' (Col. 1:19–20).

This is it, the crux, the means of our salvation and the key to his victory over death. Jesus, the 'Son of Man', interrupted his life in eternity to live on earth, to give us those marvellous teachings, to set such a wonderful example, but most of all to die.

The sacrificial system, instituted by God as the only way for people to get right with Him, tells us that without the shedding of the blood of an innocent there can be no way back to Him. Our sins and misdemeanours get in the way; our imperfections can't live with the perfection of the Creator and Sustainer of the universe.

Here's where the two worlds collide.

Men and women racked by sin and guilt, unable to find true communion with God, their heavenly father. Too many sins, too many blood sacrifices needed to cover them, no other way to find peace with their Creator.

God, motivated by love and compassion, reaches down to humanity and offers a full reconciliation by giving Himself, in the person of the Jesus of history, the man who lived among us and gave us a glimpse of God Himself, as . . . a *sacrifice*.

He took the place of all those animals slaughtered in the temple and he allowed himself to be captured, tried by the Jewish court for blasphemy and executed by the Romans: death by crucifixion, death on a cross.

> *'This is love: not that we loved God, but that he loved us and sent his Son as an atoning sacrifice for our sins' (1 Jn. 4:10).*

Such a death. This wasn't Hitler, Stalin or Saddam Hussein, who deserved it. This wasn't your average thief, villain or scoundrel who probably also deserved it. This was a man who was present at the creation of the universe, who could have called a legion of angels to stop what was happening, who had the choice to do what he wanted. He chose his death, he chose *such a death*!

He endured insults by the Roman soldiers, a crown of thorns, and the indescribable pain of crucifixion, yet he could have wiped them out with a click of his fingers. But he went to his death willingly.

Written records tell how the crucified person was usually stripped and laid on the ground with his arms spread out on the cross-bar. They were either tied or nailed to it, then the bar with the man hanging from it was lifted to be fastened to the vertical stake. After that, the feet were tied or nailed in place. Death came by suffocation, as the victim's chest muscles weakened, preventing breathing. To speed things up, the legs were broken so that he couldn't push himself up and take air into his lungs. The pain would have been indescribable.

There is a painting by Mathias Grunewald called 'The Crucifixion'. It's different to most of the others in that it pulls no punches. Here we see Jesus' dying body distorted by the torture of the cross; the thorns of the scourges stuck in the festering wounds which cover the whole figure. The dark red blood forms a glaring contrast to the sickly green of the flesh. The fingers are gnarled in death, and the face bears the imprint of the final agony of suffering. The lips are white and the eyes are sunk deep in the skull. The artist has even indicated the spit. There are pieces of metal and wood actually in the flesh.

There was also the unimaginable degradation in the manner of his death. The Jews knew that everyone who was crucified was cursed. It was a punishment reserved for criminals. The Jewish leaders taunted him: *'Save yourself, and come down from the cross and we will believe you; He saved others: himself he cannot save.'* He could have done so if he'd wanted to. But he didn't.

Jesus died for me. He died for our sins. What does this *really* mean? First, the shedding of blood was necessary for getting right with God; a sacrifice is always needed. Secondly, in some way, the death of Jesus provided this sacrifice in a way that no previous sacrifice (and there had been millions of them) had ever done. In fact, no sacrificial blood ever again had to be shed!

> *'He committed no sin, and no deceit was found in his mouth'*
> *(1 Pet. 2:22).*

It is our sin that separates us all from God. Because of this separation even Jesus, who lived a sinless life, still needed to pray to his heavenly Father during times when he found solitude. He suffered anguished separation when he cried from the cross, *'My God, my God, why have you forsaken me?'* (Mt. 27:46). Although he didn't have to, he chose to live a life of full identification with the rest of humankind, including periods of temptation, hunger, thirst, tiredness and suffering. We have absolutely no idea what that man had to go through on our behalf.

Remember *The Lion, the Witch and the Wardrobe*, by C.S. Lewis? The evil witch knew of the Deep Magic, whereby the blood of anyone in Narnia guilty of treachery belonged to her, and so she had the right to kill the boy Edmund. When Aslan took Edmund's place on the stone altar and was killed, she thought she had the victory. But Aslan knew of the *Deeper Magic*: when a willing victim without treachery (or sin) was killed on behalf of others, death would be defeated. Yes, there is a deeper magic, and when C.S. Lewis wrote of this, he had one thing in mind: the death of Jesus.

A man without sin died for our sins.

> *'For the wages of sin is death . . .'* (Rom. 6:23).

Everyone who sins tastes death, but the *deeper magic* kicks in when someone who didn't sin is put to death. It happened two thousand years ago at a cross of crucifixion, just outside Jerusalem. It jarred the system; it was a catalyst for disruption. Death was defeated by this one act. The finer workings are a mystery, a deeper magic, but things were never to be the same again. The second half of the quote provides us with the consequences of that awesome act:

> '. . . *but the gift of God is eternal life in Christ Jesus our Lord.*'

Jesus' death on the cross was God's gift to us. Get your head around that one. He defeated death, displaying this fact to the world three days later, when his resurrected body was seen by his close friends.

So Jesus had come as the divine *bar anash*, Son of Man, to redeem the people of earth, to bring them back into a living relationship with God. He had also come as *Messiah*, the anointed one, to show his people how to live. But these are just titles, aspects of the *Man of Many Names*. His titles are interchangeable; they all highlight a particular aspect of his life and character but work together to provide the complete picture. Hence the title Son of Man has also been used to emphasize his humanity to those Gentile Christians who had lost sight of this.

Also, when we consider the true nature of Messiah as the '*anointed one*', we recognize that in the Old Testament there were other anointed ones: the priests and kings, both of which roles Jesus himself fulfilled. We will look at his role as king a little later, but first we will dwell on how Jesus functioned as a priest. A complete explanation is given in the book of Hebrews, and there is no need, in this case, to venture further than the pages of the Bible:

> '*Therefore, since we have a great high priest who has gone through the heavens, Jesus the Son of God, let us hold firmly to the faith we profess*' (Heb. 4:14).

Now in Bible times the high priest, the *Kohen Gadol*, was the person designated to represent humankind in its relationship with God. For example, it was he alone who dealt with the sins of the people of God by making a sacrifice at the holy of holies in the temple once a year at Yom Kippur, the Day of Atonement. When Jesus came and made the ultimate sacrifice on the cross, he became the final and eternal high priest, atoning not just for the Jews but for the sins of the whole of humanity. No more trips were needed to the temple, at Yom Kippur or at any other time. In fact God was to make this very clear, as you will see at the start of the next chapter.

PART THREE

The Last Days

8

Mashiach ben Yosef

Question: What was the biggest mistake ever made, and how was it covered up?

Jesus had come and gone, and for the Jewish authorities life would not be the same again. In fact, their own writings in the Talmud speak of a most interesting situation concerning the temple in Jerusalem. Once a year on *Yom Kippur* (the Day of Atonement) a scarlet cord would be tied to the horn of the scapegoat as the high priest entered the temple to make his annual sacrifice for the sins of the people. Every year this cord would miraculously turn white, indicating God's acceptance of the sacrifice. This is an allusion to Isaiah 1:18:

> *' "Come now, let us reason together," says the Lord. "Though your sins are like scarlet, they shall be as white as snow; though they are red as crimson, they shall be like wool." '*

Yet something strange happened one Yom Kippur, according to the Talmud:

> *'Our Rabbis taught: During the last forty years before the*
> *destruction of the Temple the lot did not come up in the right*
> *hand; nor did the crimson-coloured strap become white.'*[1]

The temple was destroyed in AD 70. Forty years before
this would be AD 30. So from AD 30, God showed his dis-
pleasure by not accepting the annual temple sacrifice for
forgiveness of the sins of the Jewish people. What could
have happened around AD 30 to incur divine annoyance? What single event did away the need for further
sacrifices, so much so that any attempt at doing so
would be rejected?

> *'Day after day every priest stands and performs his religious*
> *duties; again and again he offers the same sacrifices, which can*
> *never take away sins. But when this priest [Jesus] had offered*
> *for all time one sacrifice for sins, he sat down at the right hand*
> *of God' (Heb. 10:11–12).*

It's remarkable that this situation should be described in
the Jewish writings, as this adds such authenticity to the
Christian position.

If proof were needed that the Jewish authorities had
got it wildly wrong in their rejection of Jesus, then this
was it. And in their own writings too. But it didn't stop
them continuing to look for their Messiah.

According to Josephus, the prominent Jewish historian of the day, a number of 'Messiahs' appeared in the
land in that period.

> *'Another body of wicked men also sprang up, cleaner in their*
> *hands, but more wicked in their intentions, who destroyed the*
> *peace of the city no less than did these murderers [the Sicarii].*
> *For they were deceivers and deluders of the people, and, under*
> *pretence of divine illumination, were for innovations and*

changes, and prevailed on the multitude to act like madmen, and went before them in the wilderness, pretending that God would there show them signs of liberty.'²

One such deluder was Theudas, said to have been even more popular than Jesus in his day, arriving on the scene about ten years after the crucifixion. He managed to gather together around four hundred followers whom he led to the River Jordan, which would have been fine if they had been there just for a good wash, or even a mass baptism. But no. Theudas saw himself as a second Moses and attempted to command the waters to part. They didn't, and the only thing that did part was his head from his body, when the Romans captured and beheaded him and many of his followers.³

Another, an Egyptian, is said to have gathered around thirty thousand followers. He brought them to the Mount of Olives, opposite Jerusalem, promising that at his command the walls of Jerusalem would fall down, and that he and his followers would enter and possess the city. But the Roman procurator saw them off. The 'Messiah' escaped but the rest were done to death.

Here were the facts. As we have already read, the prophecy from Daniel 9:25 spoke of an 'anointed one', a Messiah, who had to come in the first part of the first century and be killed around AD 30–40. Someone had to come then, otherwise Daniel was a false prophet. But the wise men from the east followed an angel (disguised as a star), the shepherds in the field were alerted by a great company of angels, and Joseph the step-dad was spoken to by another angel in a dream. The angels knew what was going on, because God had sent them on a mission.

The Daniel prophecy had kicked in, as did all the others explained in Chapter 3. A Messiah had arrived. His name was Jesus. He was crucified in Jerusalem, and as a visual aid to the unbelieving priests, not only did the curtain in the temple tear in half, but as we have seen, the scarlet cord later that year was not divinely bleached. Then around forty years later the temple was no more, all its records destroyed by the Romans, and a key qualification for Messiahship – descent from King David – rendered unproveable. For a people so familiar with the bureaucratic process, any future contender for the role of 'Messiah' could never legally prove his genealogical credentials.

So unless the rules had somehow changed, the Messiah was either never going to make an appearance, or had already come! By the time the Talmud had been compiled in the fourth century, this thought was already starting to nag at some of them. In one place it says, '*All the predestined dates for the Redemption have passed, and the matter now depends only on repentance and good deeds.*'[4] It seemed that the deadline had passed, so where was the Messiah?

Now the Jewish religious authorities had another problem. Although it was undeniable that Jesus did not fulfil all the prophecies of the Old Testament (more of that later), he went to great pains to explain to his followers which scriptures he had come to fulfil. These were the scriptures, already covered in Chapter 3, speaking of the Suffering Servant, the one born to serve and to die. So how could these scriptures be explained away by the Jewish authorities? These prophecies were totally inconsistent with their expectations, so how did they fit into the scheme of things?

Before we consider this problem, it is worthwhile examining exactly what Messiah they were looking for and are still looking for. In fact, it is worth looking now at what the Jewish religious scholars are looking for in their Messiah, and why they are adamant that Jesus failed the test.

Most religious Jews these days follow a creed called the *Ani maamin*, translated as 'I believe', written by the Rambam (Maimonides), a Jewish scholar from the Middle Ages and one of the most highly regarded of all Jewish sages. This is the thirteen Principles of Faith, the twelfth of which states:

'Ani Maamin B'emunah Sh'leimah B'viyat Hamashiach. V'af al pi sheyitmahmehah im kol zeh achake lo b'chol yom sheyavo.'

'I believe with full faith in the coming of the Messiah. And even though he tarries, with all that, I await his arrival with every day.'

Make no mistake. The Messiah is still serious business among religious Jews today. I visited a website, *Moshiach Online*, presented as the Jewish view on the Messiah, with a comprehensive treatment of every aspect of this subject.[5] It quotes the following scriptures as key to the understanding of Messiah:

'The Spirit of the LORD will rest on him – the Spirit of wisdom and of understanding, the Spirit of counsel and of power, the Spirit of knowledge and of the fear of the LORD – and he will delight in the fear of the LORD. He will not judge by what he sees with his eyes, or decide by what he hears with his ears; but with righteousness he will judge the needy, with justice he will give decisions for the poor of the earth. He will strike the earth with the rod of his mouth; with the breath of his lips he will slay the wicked. Righteousness will be his belt and faithfulness the sash around his waist. The wolf will live with the lamb, the leopard will lie down with the goat, the calf and the lion and the yearling together; and a little child will lead them' (Is. 11:2–6).

> *'He will judge between the nations and will settle disputes for many peoples. They will beat their swords into ploughshares and their spears into pruning hooks. Nation will not take up sword against nation, nor will they train for war any more'* (Is. 2:4).

The above two prophecies speak of a righteous and powerful judge, the whole earth under his command. He will abolish war and rid the world of the wicked. Clearly this person has not arrived yet and no less a 'Talmudic scholar' than Woody Allen has indicated his scepticism in his learned commentary – *'And the lamb and the wolf shall lie down together, but the lamb won't get any sleep.'*

> *'Do not be afraid, for I am with you; I will bring your children from the east and gather you from the west. I will say to the north, "Give them up!" and to the south, "Do not hold them back." Bring my sons from afar and my daughters from the ends of the earth'* (Is. 43:5–6).

The Messiah, in their view, will return the Jewish people to the land of Israel. As most Jews still live in exile (Diaspora), this has not yet happened.

> *'I will make a covenant of peace with them; it will be an everlasting covenant. I will establish them and increase their numbers, and I will put my sanctuary among them for ever. My dwelling-place will be with them; I will be their God, and they will be my people. Then the nations will know that I the LORD make Israel holy, when my sanctuary is among them for ever'* (Ezek. 37:26–28).

The Messiah, in their view, will rebuild the temple in Jerusalem. Again, this has not happened.

The rabbis have been waiting centuries for such a Messiah. For the best explanation of their expectations we turn to Maimonides, aka Rambam, who wrote:

> 'The anointed King is destined to stand up and restore the Davidic Kingdom to its antiquity, to the first sovereignty. He will build the Temple in Jerusalem and gather the strayed ones of Israel together. All laws will return in his days as they were before.'[6]

He was scathing in his examination of Jesus, particularly the aftermath of his life and ministry, even quoting from Daniel 11:14 to identify him as a renegade who stumbled:

> 'The violent men among your own people will rebel in fulfilment of the vision, but without success' (Dan. 11:14).

To Maimonides, the actions of 'Christians', rather than redeeming and ingathering the Jews, demonstrated the very reverse:

> 'Could there be a greater stumbling block than this [Jesus]? For all the prophets spoke of the Messiah who will redeem and save Israel, who will ingather all its exiles, and who will strengthen them in the fulfilment of the Torah's commandments – while he [Jesus] caused Israel to be killed by the sword, their remnants to be dispersed and humiliated, the Torah to be switched for something else, and most of the world to worship a G-d other than the G-d of Israel!'[7]

And who could blame him, in all honesty? Although Jesus himself wasn't a stumbling block, his supposed followers were. The treatment of Jewish people at the hands of Christians through events such as the Crusades

and the Inquisition was a blot on the history of humanity and had nothing in common with the teachings of
Jesus. (For a discussion of these issues please see *The
People of Many Names*.) In fact, when we consider the
massacres and expulsions committed in Jesus' name,
Maimonides hit the nail on the head when he accused
them of forcing '*most of the world to worship a G-d other
than the G-d of Israel*'. Interestingly, the quoted section
here was censored by the church and didn't appear in
editions published after 1574. Maimonides then continues in his writings to state that the world has been so
corrupted by the followers of Jesus and Muhammad that
this very situation will pave the way for the coming of
the true Messiah. How ironic!

As a result of the teachings of Maimonides, 'Messiah'
has not yet come and clearly Jesus is not the one,
because:

- He did not bring an end to wars and wicked people
- He did not lead the Jewish people back to Israel
- He did not rebuild the temple

This is the party line. This is their set response to
Christian 'missionaries'. This has been the argument
passed down from sage to sage, rabbi to rabbi, to the
current day. It is a major stumbling block preventing an
Orthodox Jew from accepting Jesus as Messiah. It is not
enough arguing from Holy Scripture, because that is
never enough. Doctrine may be based on the Hebrew
scriptures, but it is interpreted by learned sages such as
Maimonides over hundreds of years of history.

But they had a problem, a big one: how to explain
away the Suffering Servant and the scriptures that spoke
of him. The Old Testament seemed to speak of not one,
but two Promised Ones, two Messiahs of very different

character and purpose. Jesus fulfilled one and not the other. The Messiah expected by those first-century Jews was not fulfilled by Jesus during his brief sojourn on earth. So although it may have been easy for Jewish scholars then and now to say that Jesus couldn't have been the kingly, conquering Messiah, it is a lot harder for them to explain away the *other* Messiah, the Suffering Servant.

By the time the Talmud was compiled in the fourth century, they had developed an interesting concept that would address this situation. They began to talk of an individual called 'Messiah Son of Joseph', or in Hebrew, *Mashiach ben Yosef*.

This character was meant to be linked not only to the Suffering Servant of Isaiah 53, but also to other prophecies in such places as the book of Zechariah that spoke of a Messiah other than the great king and judge who will bring peace to the earth, rebuild the temple and bring back the Jews to the land. It was a fudge to explain away the prophecies fulfilled by Jesus in his first coming. After all, if it could be proved that the Jews still waited for two Messiahs, it gave strength to their argument that Jesus couldn't have been either!

Messiah Son of Joseph is to be of the tribe of Ephraim, the Son of Joseph. That immediately disqualified Jesus, of course, who belonged to the house and line of David, the *true* Messianic line. This 'Messiah' is to come first, before the second Messiah, the 'Messiah Son of David', but would have a subservient role. His role resembles that of John the Baptist, in that he would prepare the world for the coming of the main man. That's where any resemblance ends. Despite supposedly fitting the profile of a Suffering Servant, this Son of Joseph is a politician and a military man. He will wage war against Israel's enemies, particularly the descendants of Esau, whichever nation claims descent from the ancient Edomites. Here is the supporting scripture:

> *'"The house of Jacob will be a fire and the house of Joseph a flame; the house of Esau will be stubble, and they will set it on fire and consume it. There will be no survivors from the house of Esau." The LORD has spoken' (Obad. 1:18).*

There will be a massive confrontation and the Son of Joseph will be killed. This idea is supported by the scripture often attributed to Jesus:

> *'. . . and they will mourn for him as one mourns for an only child, and grieve bitterly for him as one grieves for a firstborn son' (Zech. 12:10).*

Time
of J's
Trouble

His death will be the beginning of the end, the tribulation period, which will present a series of tests for Israel. Then the Son of David will come, avenge his death and resurrect him. Then will come the Messianic era of peace and harmony.

So that's the Jewish end-time script. But there's a twist to it. You see, it's an interactive script and can go in either of two ways. If the world progresses in the current manner (i.e. a steady decline), the script will be acted out as above. But there's a second possibility, a scenario that doesn't necessarily include the Son of Joseph at all.

In short, it all depends on the spiritual condition of the Jewish people at any given time. If they return to God in a big way, there will be no need for a Son of Joseph, no tests and tribulations. Instead the Messiah Son of David will come at his allotted time to redeem his people.

For this to happen, Jewish people worldwide, from Orthodox rabbis to atheistic humanists, would unilaterally drop to their knees in deep repentance for their sins.

Isn't this ironic? This is exactly what is going to happen, according to the Christian worldview, but rather than ushering in the rule of their expected Messiah Son of David, the one who is going to appear is none other than Jesus, in his Second Coming. But they will know this because this is the very reason for their repentance; it is this realization:

> 'They will look on me, the one they have pierced, and they will mourn for him as one mourns for an only child, and grieve bitterly for him as one grieves for a firstborn son. On that day the weeping in Jerusalem will be great, like the weeping of Hadad Rimmon in the plain of Megiddo' (Zech. 12:10–11).

But the rabbis are not yet at that point of realization. Instead they look for a unilateral repentance of the Jewish people worldwide. As there's as much likelihood of this happening as the Pope converting to Judaism, it's the other scenario the rabbis are looking towards. The passage they refer to here is in the Talmud:

> 'The Holy One, blessed be He, will set up a ruler over them, whose decrees shall be as cruel as Haman's, thus causing Israel to repent, and thereby bringing them back to the right path.'[8]

So the view of these religious Jews is that the Son of Joseph will figure in some way in end-time events. But there are further options, in the grey area between these two main scenarios. The severity of the tribulations depends on how the Jews respond to the Son of Joseph. If they respond well, there will perhaps be a minor flood and a border skirmish or two. If his efforts are in vain, perhaps a major earthquake or two and the nuclear option.

Ironically, this title, 'Messiah Son of Joseph', speaks far more of Jesus than it does of this future warrior Messiah.

They were referring to the Joseph of the (supposed) multi-coloured dreamcoat, son of Jacob, sold into slavery by his brothers but who became Pharaoh's right-hand man. Many ancient rabbis saw in the life of Joseph a picture of the Suffering Servant, so much so that this first Messiah was to be named after him. So why the comparison?

It's very useful to look at the life of Joseph and to see how it mirrors not just the Suffering Servant of Isaiah 53 but also, more interestingly, the life of Jesus.

Both were loved by their fathers:

> *'Now Israel loved Joseph more than any of his other sons'*
> *(Gen. 37:3).*

> *'And a voice from heaven said, "This is my Son, whom I love; with him I am well pleased"' (Mt. 3:17).*

But both were hated by their brothers:

> *'When his brothers saw that their father loved him more than any of them, they hated him and could not speak a kind word to him' (Gen. 37:4).*

> *'But now they have seen these miracles, and yet they have hated both me and my Father. But this is to fulfil what is written in their Law: "They hated me without reason"' (Jn. 15:24–25).*

Both were victims of a conspiracy by their enemies to put them to death:

> *'But they saw him in the distance, and before he reached them, they plotted to kill him' (Gen. 37:18).*

> *'Then the Pharisees went out and began to plot with the Herodians how they might kill Jesus' (Mk. 3:6).*

Both went to Egypt in their youth:

> *'Now Joseph had been taken down to Egypt' (Gen. 39:1).*

> *'So he got up, took the child and his mother during the night and left for Egypt' (Mt. 2:14).*

Both began their ministry at the age of thirty:

> *'Joseph was thirty years old when he entered the service of Pharaoh king of Egypt' (Gen. 41:46).*

> *'Now Jesus himself was about thirty years old when he began his ministry' (Lk. 3:23).*

This is just a taster, but it is very possible to find more and more startling similarities, the closer you look. Read the story of Joseph again through 'Gospel eyes' and see what I mean.

Notes

1. Yoma 39b.
2. William Whiston, *The Works of Josephus* (Hendrickson, 1995), p. 614.
3. Ibid. p. 531.
4. Sanhedrin 97b.
5. http://www.moshiach.com
6. His views on the Messiah are discussed in Mishneh Torah, his 14-volume commentary on the Torah, in the section *Hilkhot Melakhim – The Laws of Kings*, chapter 11.
7. *The Laws of Kings*, 11,4.
8. Sanhedrin 97b.

9

Yeshu HaNotzri

Question: How was the real Jesus hidden from ordinary
Jews for nearly 1,500 years?

The question posed at the head of the previous chapter was subsequently answered. But I will spell it out
clearly now, anyway. The failure by the Jewish leadership to recognize Jesus as Messiah two thousand
years ago was just about the biggest mistake made by
anyone in the history of the world. It was a mistake
that was to have historical consequences, starting
with the destruction of the temple in Jerusalem in AD
70, tragically witnessed by some of the generation
who had possibly seen the rejection and crucifixion of
Jesus some forty years earlier. This was at the hands of
the pagan Romans and Jesus had, in fact, prophesied
it.

> *'Jesus left the temple and was walking away when his disciples*
> *came up to him to call his attention to its buildings. "Do you*
> *see all these things?" he asked. "I tell you the truth, not one*
> *stone here will be left on another; every one will be thrown*
> *down"' (Mt. 24:1–2).*

Then, when the first fires of Christian zeal, righteousness and faithfulness had been squeezed out of the church by the compromises forced on it by its adoption by what was left of the Roman Empire, a full programme of painful circumstances was inflicted on the Jewish people. This was at the hands of a vengeful church acting out of misplaced zeal for a vengeful God, who existed nowhere but in their own vengeful hearts.

It became clear to the Jewish religious leaders that they had made the right decision to hold on to the 'ways of their fathers' and not embrace this new religious system that seemed so full of self-righteous hate. *God forbid that we should become like one of them*! They retreated inwards, into the sureties of their scriptures and the proclamations of their sages, who demonstrably led holy lives consistent with their calling, a stark contrast to the popes and bishops who openly preached hate and vengeance and who mobilized armies to carry out their devilish schemes.

It was no wonder that Jews clung to their beliefs to the point of death, and they should not be ridiculed or condemned for it. It was no wonder that so few became followers of Jesus the Messiah, when the only visible witness to him was at the point of a sword or the lick of a flame. It was no wonder that their religious teachers constructed a body of work to make it difficult, or well-nigh impossible, to ever contemplate 'going over to the dark side'.

They struck back hard, in the only way they could, through religious proclamations, ordinances and commentary. A Jew professing to follow Jesus was to be considered a Jew no more by the Jewish community. He was judged to have committed one of the three cardinal sins, alongside murder and incest.[1] This was no joking matter, and still is, even to this day. To back up these extreme views, the rabbis embarked on a campaign of misinformation and vilification to strike at the heart of the Christian faith. The target was the very person of Jesus himself.

The *Amidah* is the most important collection of prayers spoken daily by Jews worldwide. It consists of eighteen prayers, a collection built up through the centuries since the destruction of the temple in Jerusalem in AD 70. Each prayer has a name and each has a separate function. The first praises God and thanks Him for the patriarchs. The second offers praise to God for His great power. The third praises God for His holiness. The fourth asks God for wisdom and understanding. The fifth praises God for gifting us with repentance. The sixth praises God for His forgiveness. The seventh praises Him as the redeemer of Israel. The eighth is a prayer for healing. The ninth asks God to bless the produce of the earth. The tenth asks God to allow the Jews to return to Israel. The eleventh asks God to raise up righteous judges. And the twelfth?

The twelfth prayer or benediction is called *Birkat HaMinim* and it asks God to destroy those in 'heretical sects'. So not so much a blessing as a curse. It was added to the Amidah around the time of the Greek occupation of Judea and Samaria, directed at those Jews who had compromised and followed Greek ways. It was in the first century AD that the prayer came to prominence, revised by Samuel ha-Katan (Samuel the Small), as a direct provocation to those Jews who followed Jesus, yet still used in the synagogues.

The story is told in the Talmud:

> 'Rabban Gamaliel said to the sages, "Is there anyone who knows how to compose a 'Blessing' about the heretics?" Samuel the Small stood up and composed it. The following year he forgot it, and tried to recall it for two and even three

hours, yet they still did not call him down from the pulpit.
Why did they not call him down? Because Rab Judah cited Rab
as saying, that "If a man makes a mistake in any of the daily
'Blessings', they do not call him down. But if he makes a mis-
take in the Blessing against the heretics, they do call him
down." [This is because] they then suspect him of being a
heretic. But if was different in the case of Samuel the Small,
because he had composed it, and it was thought that maybe he
could remember [if he had enough time]."²

Yes, it is hard going, but the gist of it is that Rabbi
Gamaliel II, the grandson of the Gamaliel who taught
Paul, was eager for someone to compose a prayer
against those who professed Christianity. Samuel the
Small stepped forward and obliged. This had to be the
parting of the ways, as no Jewish believers in Jesus, considered slanderers at that time, would recite the prayer:

'*May the slanderers have no hope; and may all wickedness per-*
ish in an instant; and may all of our enemies be cut down
speedily. May you speedily uproot, smash, cast down and
humble the arrogant sinners – speedily in our days. Blessed
are You, O Lord, who breaks enemies and humbles arrogant
sinners.'

Jewish Christians were even known as *minim*, heretics,
by their estranged brethren. Other names given to them
by Jewish religious leaders include *apikoresim* (heretics)
or *meshummadin* (apostates), but it was the names given
to Jesus himself that really raised the ante.

The names given presented Jesus in an immoral light,
as illegitimate (though one can see where that one came
from), as self-centred, as an idolater and a blasphemer.
The Talmud referred to him as *Yeshu*, which may seem
an affectionate shortening of his Hebrew name, Yeshua,

but in fact was an acronym for the Hebrew expression *yemach shemo vezichro*, which means, 'May his name and memory be obliterated.' In many places the full name used is *Yeshu HaNotzri*, the second word meaning 'the Nazarene'. Interestingly, the Catholics ordered the rabbis to remove the name from the Talmud, which is why it is only found in ancient versions of the Jewish writings.

There is another variation of this name in the ancient writings: *Yeshu ben Pandera*, meaning Yeshu son of Pandera. Pandera was meant to be the name of Mary's lover, a carnal dig at the Virgin Birth. A curious embellishment is the insistence that Mary was a women's hairdresser, though this is likely to be a mistranslation, a literary variation of Chinese whispers. Pandera, sometimes nicknamed Stada, was thought to be a Roman soldier. This whole scenario reeks of spitefulness, as if the fabricator intended to present the most shameful and disrespectful situation he could think of. This is the very thing that sets the seal of falsehood on the matter, and it is hard to believe that anyone actually believed these lies.

In all, over twenty different 'nicknames' for Jesus appear in Jewish writing. One of these is *otho ha'ish*, or 'that man', or 'that certain person' or 'so-and-so'. None of these names is endearing; all are a reaction to what was happening to Jewish communities throughout the known world at the hands of those who professed to follow 'that man'. The most popular theme plays on the fact of his being of illegitimate birth, a *mamzer*, as we can see from the following:

> 'Rabbi Shimon ben Azai said, "I have found a roll of pedigrees in Jerusalem, and therein is written, A certain person is of spurious birth; to confirm the words of Rabbi Yehoshua."'[3]

'A certain person', as mentioned above, is one of the oblique names for Jesus in the Talmud, and the reference to his spurious birth is an allusion to his parentage. According to the Talmud, one who was born out of wedlock (as it seemed with Jesus) was condemned to a judicial death, so his fate would have been sealed long before his ministry got started.

Some of the fiercest attacks on Jesus in the Talmud were concerned with his miracles. The fact of them was not denied; instead the focus was on their source. A medieval document, *Toledot Yeshu* ('The History/Generations of Jesus'), claimed to be an account of the life of Jesus, but was just a fabricated string of insults. It was a reaction to the extreme pain and persecution brought about at the hands of the church and was deeply prejudiced against Jesus. It insisted that he performed his miracles by abusing the power of God's name. Here is an extract:

> 'In the Temple was to be found the Foundation Stone on which were engraved the letters of God's Ineffable Name. Whoever learned the secret of the Name and its use would be able to do whatever he wished. Therefore the Sages took measures so that no one should gain its knowledge. Lions of brass were bound to two iron pillars at the Temple gate . . . Should anyone enter and learn the Name, when he left the lions would roar at him and immediately the valuable secrets would be forgotten.
>
> 'Yeshu came and learned the letters of the Name; he wrote them upon the parchment which he placed in an open cut on his thigh and then drew the flesh over the parchment. As he left, the lions roared and he forgot the secret. But when he came to his house he reopened the cut in his flesh with a knife and lifted out the writing. Then he remembered and obtained the use of the letters.'[4]

It was supposedly through the use of these letters that Jesus was able to perform miracles such as healing people who had leprosy or were lame.

If you think that 'taster' is bad enough, here is the 'Gospel according to Toledot Yeshu':

> *'A certain John was engaged to Mary in Bethlehem, but she betrayed him one Sabbath with a handsome villain named Joseph Pandera. John then fled to Babylon and Mary gave birth to Yeshu. He grew up as an impudent and disrespectful child and eventually fled to Jerusalem. Once he had stolen the Ineffable Name, he gathered together a group of followers in Bethlehem and proclaimed himself the Messiah, the Son of God. He performed miracles by sorcery and even raised up a dead man. He soon had a rival, a sage called Yehuda, who also stole the Ineffable Name and they were summoned to appear before the Queen. They demonstrated their powers by flying, but Yehuda flew the highest, so Yeshu was condemned to death. He was imprisoned in Tiberias but was rescued by his disciples and fled first to Antioch, then to Egypt, where he lost the Ineffable Name. So he returned to Jerusalem to steal it again but he was captured, imprisoned, then hanged to death on a cabbage stem. His body was subsequently stolen from his tomb by a gardener and his disciples declared that he had been restored to life. The Queen was fooled by this and sentenced the Sages of Israel to death, but they were reprieved when someone found the corpse, tied it to the tail of a horse and brought it to the Queen.'*[5]

You couldn't make it up! Well, they did, and it was not so much 'spot the mistakes' as search for any crumbs of truth! Intriguingly, there is the odd snippet of familiarity sprinkled throughout this yarn, but all in the wrong order and context.

It is significant that the *Toledot Yeshu* became the chief source of information about Jesus for the Jews of eastern Europe from the early Middle Ages to the early twentieth century. It may have been a means of fighting back internally against the massive threat from outside, fuelled by rampant anti-Semitism, but all it did was ensure that more Jewish minds were closed to the glorious truths of the Gospel.

In terms of his teachings, Jesus was called a fool in the Talmud because of his claim to be the Son of God. The Talmud also asserts that Jesus was an idolater, particularly in the section that makes the most mention of him, Sanhedrin 103a. Here is an example:

> '"Neither shall any plague come nigh your tent" (Ps. 91:10); in other words, you shall have no son or disciple who burns his food publicly, like Jesus the Nazarene.'

The expression 'burns his food' refers to apostasy, probably a contemptuous remark alluding to the public offering of a sacrifice to idols.

Elsewhere it is declared '*Jesus practised sorcery, and corrupted and seduced Israel.*'[6] And Sanhedrin 107b elaborates on this by reciting a story of how another rabbi was reciting the *Shema* when Jesus approached him. The rabbi beckoned him, but Jesus misread his intention and walked away and worshipped an idol. The rabbi called out to him but Jesus responded with false teaching. The conclusion of this story is that '*Jesus the Nazarene practised magic and led astray and deceived Israel.*'

Although the Talmud did not deny the crucifixion as a historical fact, the reasons for it were altered:

> 'And it is tradition: On the eve of the Passover Yeshu the Nazarene was hung. But the herald went forth before him

> *for the space of forty days, while he cried, "Yeshu the Nazarene goes forth to be stoned, because he has practised sorcery and seduced Israel and led them astray. Let anyone who knows anything in his favour come forward and give information concerning it." But no plea was found for him, and so he was hung on the eve of Passover. Ulla said, "But do you think that there could be anything in his favour? He was a seducer, and the All Merciful has said, 'You shall not spare him, nor conceal him' (Deut. 13:8)." However, in Jesus' case it was different, because he was near to the kingdom.'[7]*

They would have liked to stone him for his alleged blasphemy, but the fact is that they didn't; the Romans had rendered them powerless. This is why Jesus was crucified: it was a Roman punishment.

This passage in the Talmud goes on to talk about Jesus' disciples. It makes interesting and baffling reading:

> 'Our Rabbis have taught, Jesus had five disciples – Matthai, Nekai, Netzer, Buni, and Thodah. They brought Matthai [before the judges]. He said, "Must Matthai be killed? For it is written (Ps. 42:2), 'Matthai [i.e., 'when'] shall [I] come and appear before God.'" They said to him, "Yes, Matthai must be killed, for it is written (Ps. 41:5), 'Matthai [i.e., 'when'] shall [he] die and his name perish.'" They brought Nekai. He said to them, "Must Nekai be killed? For it is written (Ex. 23:7), 'The Naki [i.e., 'innocent'] and the righteous you shall not slay.'" They said to him, "Yes, Nekai must be killed, for it is written (Ps. 10:8), 'In secret places does he slay Naki [i.e., 'the innocent'].'" They brought Netzer. He said, "Must Netzer be killed? For it is written (Is. 11:1), 'Netzer [i.e., 'a branch'] shall spring up from his roots.'" They said to him, "Yes, Netzer must be killed. For it is written (Is. 14:19), 'You are cast forth out of*

your grave like an abominable Netzer [i.e., 'branch'].'" They brought Buni. He said to them, "Must Buni be killed? For it is written (Ex. 4:22), 'Buni [i.e., 'my son'], my firstborn, Israel.'" They said to him, "Yes, Buni must be killed. For it is written (Ex. 4:23), 'Behold, I slay Bincha [i.e., 'your son'], your first born.'" They brought Thodah. He said to them, "Must Thodah be killed? For it is written (Ps. 100:1), 'A Psalm for Thodah [i.e., 'thanksgiving'].'" They said to him, "Yes, Thodah must be killed, for it is written (Ps. 1:23), 'Whoever sacrifices Thodah [i.e., 'thanksgiving'] honours me.'"'

Each so-called disciple has his character assassinated before actual execution. There is nothing here that smacks of any historical truth, whether through the Gospels or Christian tradition.

Yet in other places there are vague and grudging references to Jesus and his legacy if you dig deep enough. Here's an interesting passage:

'The grandson [of R. Yehoshua ben Levi] had something stuck in his throat. There came a man and whispered to him in the name of Yeshu Pandera, and he recovered. When he [the doctor] came out, he [R. Yehoshua] said to him, "What did you whisper to him?" He said to him, "A certain word." He said, "It had been better for him that he had died than thus." And it happened to him, "as it were an error that proceeded from the ruler" (Ecc. 10:5).'[8]

So: an acknowledged Christian healing in the name of Jesus, in the Talmud. The balance is redressed when we see the astonishing attack on the Trinity in this extract from the Midrash:

'R. Shmuel bar Nachman, in the name of R. Jonathan, said, When Moses was writing the Torah, he wrote the deeds of each

> *day [of creation]. When he came to this verse [Gen. 1:26],*
> *"And God said, Let Us make man in Our image, according to*
> *Our likeness," he said, "Lord of the World, how you are giv-*
> *ing a chance to the Minim! I am astonished!" He said to him,*
> *"Write; and he who will err, let him err!"*[9]

It's almost in the form of a joke, and is an acknowledgement by the rabbis of the plurality in Genesis 1:26 that
implies the Trinity. Another attack is seen here, in a commentary on Daniel 3, the story of the three men cast into
the furnace. It's an apologetic for the fact that
Nebuchadnezzar uses the embarrassing (for them)
phrase 'Son of God'.

> *'[Dan 3:25] "Like a son of God." Reuben said, In that hour, an*
> *angel descended and struck that wicked one [Nebuchadnezzar]*
> *upon his mouth, and said to him, Amend your words. Has He*
> *a son? He turned and said [verse 28] "Blessed be the God of*
> *Shadrach, Meshach, and Abednego, who — it is not written,*
> *'has sent his son', but — has sent his angel, and has delivered*
> *his servants who trusted in him."*[10]

Now let's put all this into context. The Talmud was full
of less than complimentary references to Jesus. It was
just about the only way the Jewish scholars and sages
could fight back against the ominous rise of a
Christianity that seemed hell-bent on wiping the Jewish
nation from the face of the earth. If they couldn't fight
back in the traditional sense, then at least they could do
their utmost to ensure that current and future generations of Jews would be persuaded against joining the
enemy. By making Jesus seem such an unsavoury character, they probably largely succeeded.

But even this weapon was eventually taken away
from them. The Christians caught on, and in Paris in

1244 the first copies of the Talmud were burnt, after a public disputation between Jews and Christians.

This may, or may not, have been what went on in that disputation . . .

The Pope decided that all the Jews had to leave the Vatican. Naturally there was a big uproar from the Jewish community. So the Pope made a deal. He would have a religious debate with a member of the Jewish community. If the Jew won, the Jews could stay. If the Pope won, the Jews would leave. The Jews realized that they had no choice. So they picked a middle-aged man named Moishe to represent them. Moishe asked for one addition to the debate. To make it more interesting, neither side would be allowed to talk. The Pope agreed.

The day of the great debate came. Moishe and the Pope sat opposite each other for a full minute before the Pope raised his hand and showed three fingers. Moishe looked back at him and raised one finger. The Pope waved his fingers in a circle around his head. Moishe pointed to the ground where he sat. The Pope pulled out a wafer and a glass of wine. Moishe pulled out an apple. The Pope stood up and said, 'I give up. This man is too good. The Jews can stay.'

An hour later, the cardinals were all round the Pope asking him what had happened. The Pope said, 'First I held up three fingers to represent the Trinity. He responded by holding up one finger to remind me that there was still one God common to both our religions. Then I waved my finger around me to show him that God was all around us. He responded by pointing to the ground and showing that God was also right here with us. I pulled out the wine and the wafer to show that God absolves us from our sins. He pulled out an apple to remind me of original sin. He had an answer for everything. What could I do?'

Meanwhile, the Jewish community had crowded round Moishe. 'What happened?' they asked. 'Well,' said Moishe, 'First he said to me that the Jews had three days to get out of here. I told him that not one of us was leaving. Then he told me that this whole city would be cleared of Jews. I let him know that we were staying right here.' 'And then?' asked a woman. 'I don't know,' said Moishe. 'He took out his lunch and I took out mine.'

On the other hand, perhaps it didn't happen quite in that way (in fact it's a joke, in case you are wondering!).

There were further attacks against the Talmud in a Papal Bull in 1264, with the first attempt at censoring those passages that spoke against Jesus and Christianity. This came to a head in 1413, in Tortosa, when another Papal Bull, this time by Pope Martin V, went as far as forbidding Jews from reading it, though this was largely ignored. The Talmud that was printed in Venice in 1520 was actually produced under the protection of the Vatican.

Yet the Catholic Church was still not happy, and thirty years later it began a new campaign of Talmud-burning. It was the time of the Inquisition, when burning of their holy books was the least of the Jews' problems. More burnings and censorships ensued, culminating in Pope Pius IV's command in 1565 that the Talmud should even be deprived of its name. From then on it was allegedly to be referred to as 'that book formerly known as the Talmud'.

The brand new expurgated, censored and spring-cleaned edition of the Talmud appeared in Basel from 1578. All passages deemed disrespectful of Jesus and Christianity were removed or altered by the thought police. This didn't satisfy Popes Gregory XIII and Clement VIII, who ordered a fresh wave of attacks on it and prohibitions from reading it. And from then on, wherever Jews and the Talmud could be found, controversy and persecutions followed.

The whole episode reeks of desperation. The learned sages had compiled the Talmud from thousands of years of Jewish oral tradition. That they were reduced to such pettiness and falsehood in order to discredit the founder of the religion that persecuted them mercilessly has a particular sadness. The actions of the Catholics, who burned the Talmud, prohibited Jews from reading it, and doctored it when that failed to work, were just as vindictive as those of extreme Muslims of today who are provoked into the same passions by any perceived attacks on their founder.

Notes

[1] Sanhedrin 74a.

[2] Berakoth 28b,29a.

[3] Mishnah Yevamot 4:13.

[4] Morris Goldstein, *Jesus in the Jewish Tradition* (Macmillan, 1950), p. 148–54.

[5] Based on the story in Joseph Klausner, *Jesus of Nazareth* (Menorah Publishing Co., 1979), p. 48–50.

[6] Sanhedrin 43a.

[7] Sanhedrin 43a.

[8] Jerusalem Talmud, Shabbat 14d.

[9] Genesis Rabbah 8, p. 22d.

[10] Jerusalem Talmud, Shabbat 8d.

10

Haver

Question: How did some Jews find Jesus against all the odds?

Despite the Jews' experience of centuries of hatred and persecution at the hands of his professed followers, and despite their centuries of conditioning by their own sages and scholars, Jesus has still found a way into the hearts of some Jewish people. This is a true miracle in the light of Jewish history, but doubly so when we examine the lives of those religious Jews, Talmudic scholars and even rabbis who discovered Jesus for themselves. Their stories are astonishing in the light of the battles fought over their minds and bodies in the name of this same person, the unmentionable one, whose name was nothing more than a curse to them. What a bondage to be released from! What amazing testimonies they must have had. What hardships they must have incurred, expelled from their communities and families in what would have been seen as the ultimate betrayal. It was akin to escaping from a concentration camp, only to join the Nazis as a storm trooper. Not just joining the enemy, but promoting their cause and working to seduce others into their new beliefs. So, stories of such people are not to be taken lightly. Here are a few who overcame all obstacles in order to be able to call Jesus a *Haver*, a friend.

David Baron (1855–1926)

David was born into a religious family in Russia. He was aware of God from an early age, understanding his need for reconciliation with his Maker. When he examined his heart he found, in his own words, nothing but 'blackness of darkness'. His soul was on a search, and despite keeping all the laws and ceremonies of the rabbis and the Talmud, he was restless. He had an early sense of the futility of his good works and religious observances, because they were done out of religious duty rather than love of his Creator. The more religious he became, the more miserable he was. He prayed for something more, the 'right spirit' and the 'new heart' that King David himself yearned for. So he consulted others, who told him not to worry: he was a good Jew, what more could he do?

His knowledge of the Bible became a condemnation for him. He knew that '*the soul who sins is the one who will die*' (Ezek. 18:20) and that '*it is the blood that makes atonement for one's life*' (Lev. 17:11). Where could he find that forgiveness for his sins that he ached for? He yearned for the burden to lift, but without reconciliation with God he could find no relief in the religious system he was born into.

When he was young he had a serious accident and nearly died. This terrified him and he begged his mother for reassurance. His mother responded, '*You have been such a good boy, and should you die you will go to heaven.'* This did not impress him and he rebuked her, saying, *'I have not been good, and if my getting to heaven depends on my own goodness I shall never get there.'* His was a tortured childhood.

But God had a plan for him and brought him into contact with two Christians: a Jew and a Gentile. They spoke to him of a Saviour, but at the mention of his name, David was filled with hatred and prejudice. No wonder really, as his only knowledge of Jesus was one who urged his followers to serve idols and persecute the Jews. From the age of 4 he was taught by his mother to say, whenever he passed a church, *'Utterly abhor and detest it, for it is set apart for destruction'* (Deut. 7:26). He was taught that Christianity is for Gentiles, and so to meet a Jew who professed to believe in Jesus was startling and disconcerting. His conclusion was that the man must have been bribed!

Yet this apostate, this *meshumed*, seemed happy and contented and had a peace and an assurance that David had yearned for throughout his life. In one conversation, the Jewish believer confessed, *'As for me, I tell you honestly, as in the sight of God, that I have never known what true happiness is until I found it in Christ.'* David tried his best, using his knowledge of the Hebrew scriptures and the Talmud to argue against the Messiahship of Jesus, but the one stumbling block was the evident happiness such a belief had brought to this man.

Soon afterwards, David read the New Testament for the first time. The words exploded at him. Having been brought up to believe that Jesus of Nazareth was a false prophet, he now found this man in fact teaching people to worship the One God, the only living and true God, the God of Abraham, Isaac and Jacob, the God of Israel. Of particular impact were the words of Jesus, *'Worship the Lord your God, and serve him only'* (Mt. 4:10). The following section, the Sermon on the Mount, simply blew him away. As he continued to read, he came to the realization that '*this man spoke as never man spake!*' Yet this was the man that the Talmud spoke of as 'the greatest sinner in Israel'.

David was nothing if not thorough. Without any help or counselling, he read and examined the New Testament over a period of twelve months, analysing it and comparing it with the Old Testament. Yet the effect of this was to burden his heart even more as he came to the realization that salvation can only be obtained as a gift from God through faith in Jesus Christ, and that his own righteousness apart from this salvation availed nothing in the sight of God.

His training and upbringing gradually unravelled as he considered his prayer life, his strict observance of the ceremonies prescribed by the rabbis and his study of the Talmud. It all seemed so easy: to be saved *just* by faith in Christ? What about his years of training and learning. Did they count for nothing? Yet still he clung on. '*Oh, my God!*' he cried, '*cast me not away from Thy presence in this manner. I am a Jew, a child of Abraham, Thy friend; from my youth I have tried to keep Thy holy law. Why dost Thou thus punish me, withholding from me that peace and rest of heart without which life is a burden to me? Hide not Thy face from me, lest I be as those who go down to the pit!*' And still no peace came.

Gradually his ingrained hatred of the Name of Jesus broke down, as the scriptures sank in. Did not Jesus show nothing but love to the Jews? Did he not weep over Jerusalem? Was he not moved with compassion for them? Did he not even pray for his murderers on the very cross on which they crucified him?

One day, he just gave in. In his own words he explains:

> *'By the help of God's Spirit, I cast myself on my knees one evening and exclaimed, "Oh, my God, if Thou canst not save me on any other condition but faith in Jesus, be pleased to give me that faith, and help me to love that most precious Name which I have so long hated and despised. Thou hast promised to save unto the uttermost all those who come unto Thee in His Name: Oh, save me!" I remained on my knees some time and, when I rose, I could indeed sing, "O, LORD, I will praise Thee: though Thou wast angry with me, Thine anger is turned away, and Thou comfortedst me. Behold, God is my salvation; I will trust, and not be afraid: for the LORD JEHOVAH is my Strength and my Song; He also is become my Salvation" (Is. 12:1–2, KJV).'*

David Baron became a mighty man of God. Having worked with missions to Jews, he co-founded the Hebrew Christian Testimony to Israel in 1893, in Whitechapel, London. Among the books he wrote are *The Ancient Scriptures for the Modern Jew*, *The Visions and Prophecies of Zechariah*, and *Types, Psalms and Prophecies*.

(The following biographies are adapted from material presented on the website www.shalom.org.uk.)

Rabbi Leopold Cohn (1862–1937)

Leopold learnt to trust in God from an early age, having lost both parents at the age of 7. Living in an Orthodox community in Hungary, he had his life mapped out for him, and at the age of 18 he had graduated with distinction from the Talmudic academy with a view to training to be a rabbi for his people. He was ordained and married, living in his wife's parents' home in order to have time to devote to the sacred writings and contemplation of the burning issues of his people, such as that of the exile and the long-delayed redemption through the coming of the Messiah. He prayed for this daily, often in a midnight vigil of prayer of mourning over the destruction of the temple and imploring God to hasten the coming of the Messiah of Israel.

His studies in the Talmud brought him to the conclusion that the Messiah was late: he should already have come. Yet here were the Jews, still in exile. He asked himself, '*Can it be possible that the time appointed by God for the coming of the Messiah has passed and the promise has not been fulfilled?*' For further illumination he turned to the prophets, in particular the book of Daniel, where he read the prophecy of the seventy weeks in chapter 9. It seemed to be predicting the coming of the Messiah at a time long since past. Yet there was not a word on this in the Talmud, and from that time onwards he began to question the reliability of that book. The prayer that rose to his lips at that time was, '*Open Thou mine eyes, O Lord, that I may behold wondrous things in Thy law.*'

These doubts soon got him into trouble, as he could not remain silent about them and his community reacted negatively towards him. A fellow rabbi, senior in years, rebuked him, pouring scorn on the very idea that a rabbi so tender in years could cast doubts on the teachings of the learned sages. Discredited, he travelled to America in March 1892 to seek a new life and some answers, and he was warmly welcomed by the Hungarian community in New York.

One day he chanced upon a church that announced, in Hebrew, a meeting for Jews. He was intrigued, but was warned off the place by others who said, '*There are apostate Jews in that church and they teach that the Messiah has already come.*' Rather than deterring him, these words attracted him and he secretly entered the building. A couple of days later he met up with the minister, a Jew who was a trained Talmudist with an impressive rabbinic pedigree. He was given a Hebrew New Testament to read. He opened it to the very first scripture, in Matthew. *'This is the book of the generation of Yeshua the Messiah, the son of David, the son of Abraham.'* The words spoke into his very soul.

Later on, locked away in his room, he wrote,

> *'I began reading at eleven o'clock in the morning and contin-ued until one o'clock after midnight. I could not understand the entire contents of the book, but I could at least see that the Messiah's name was Yeshua, that He was born in Bethlehem of Judah, that He had lived in Jerusalem and communicated with my people, and that He came just at the time predicted in the prophecy of Daniel. My joy was boundless.'*

His problems came when he tried to share his discovery. One rabbi snatched the New Testament from his grasp and trampled on it, saying, *'A learned rabbi like you should not even handle, much less read this vile production of the apostates. It is the cause of all our sufferings.'* Rabbi Cohn was filled with doubts and guilt, scared that he might have slipped into idolatry in contemplating this Jesus of the Gentiles! These thoughts stayed with him for days, but he was saved by his study of the scriptures, in par-ticular Isaiah 53, which spoke of the suffering Messiah. Yet he was still troubled. How shall I love the 'hated one'? How shall I defile my lips with the name of Jesus, whose followers have tortured and killed my brethren through many generations? How can I join a community of people so hostile to those of my own flesh and blood?

His next step was to fast and pray until God provided some answers. An answer came, in the book of Malachi, chapter 3:

'Behold I send my messenger, and he shall prepare the way before me, and the Lord whom ye seek shall suddenly come to His temple, even the Angel of the Covenant whom ye delight in: behold He has already come, saith the Lord of Hosts' (translation unknown).

He has already come? A sudden realization washed through his body and he fell on his face and gave his very being to the Lord Jesus. As if in direct response, a flood of light filled his understanding, and to his unspeakable happiness he no longer found it difficult to love his Lord; all barriers to the reality of Jesus were removed.

Such revelation couldn't be kept to himself, and he began to proclaim to all his friends and acquaintances that the rejected Jesus was the true Messiah of Israel, and that not until the Jews as a people accepted him could they find peace with God. First they laughed at his 'mental confusion', then persecution began against this 'traitor to his people'. They wrote to his wife and friends in Hungary, informing them of his apostasy, and he met such hostility that he had to leave New York, aided by the minister who had given him his first New Testament. He moved to Edinburgh, in Scotland, where he was baptized. Leopold was no longer a rabbi of the law, but a messenger of the Messiah, and he carried in his heart the secret of Israel's salvation.

The following year he returned to New York, a man with a mission. He immediately set about establishing contact with the Jewish community, opening a little mission building in Brownsville. He met with inevitable hostility, and the early days were difficult indeed. Here is an incident, described in his own words, that illustrates this:

'One afternoon I went to deliver a New Testament at a house where it had been requested. But when I arrived there, a powerful

> *man fell upon me, first battering me with his fists and then jump-*
> *ing upon me with his feet. Finally he took hold of my ears, and lift-*
> *ing my head, he began to knock it repeatedly against the hard*
> *floor, all the while intoning in Hebrew, "These ears which heard*
> *from Sinai that we must have no strange gods, and which now lis-*
> *ten to the Christian idols, must be pulled out," and emphasising*
> *each mention of the words "pulled out" with a terrible jerk.'*

From this experience Cohn went home with blood on his face, but it was the blood of one who had suffered for the truth's sake and it became the seed of a great work.

He persevered and, despite opposition even from other Christians, built up a large congregation of Jews whom he had won to the faith of the Messiah. Dr Leopold Cohn passed away on 19 December 1937. His funeral service at the Marcy Avenue Baptist Church in Brooklyn drew a large attendance of friends and admirers, both Jews and Christians.

Rabbi 'Chaim' Rudolf Hermann Gurland (1831–1905)

Another Jew with his life mapped out for him, Chaim was the son of a Lithuanian rabbi. Conversant with the scriptures from a very early age, he once ran away from home in order to be taken into heaven like Elijah. When of age, he became a rabbi, but reluctantly so, as even then he had begun to doubt the true worth of the Talmud in God's eyes. This became his undoing, and he had to resign his calling after publicly preaching against the Talmud and challenging others to join him.

A New Testament was given to him, though it raised more questions than answers until he was able to learn more through the efforts of a pastor working with the Jewish people in Kishinev. Pastor Faltin offered him

German lessons if he would help him in his study of Hebrew by reading through the Hebrew Bible with him every week.

The crunch came when they reached Isaiah 53, the chapter that speaks of the Suffering Servant. Chaim requested that they skip this chapter but the pastor held firm. From that time the rabbi could not help thinking about that remarkable chapter, and felt it was cowardly to be afraid to know what God had revealed in it. So he gave in, and the following week the pastor used the occasion to demonstrate the Christian view of that passage. First of all he read to him the story of Christ's sufferings as contained in the New Testament. After that they read Isaiah 53 and Chaim was forced to admit that the chapter was a perfect picture of what Jesus had suffered and acquired for us at Calvary.

To cut a long story short, this led to the baptism of Chaim (and his wife).

The day did not pass without trouble, though. Many Jews had written to him to tell him what a disgrace this public proclamation would be for the Jewish population. Others threatened to kill him at the service. The pastor even asked him whether he would prefer a quieter, more discreet ceremony, but he refused, saying, '*Jesus the Messiah is a living, mighty Saviour. He can protect me; but even if he does not, I am willing to suffer and die for him.*' The church was packed with Christians and Jews and the service proceeded without incident. After the service an elderly lady told Chaim that for eighteen years she had prayed to God and pleaded with him to save his soul.

Chaim, now called Rudolf, was ordained as a Protestant pastor. That day he preached on Romans 1:16: '*For I am not ashamed of the gospel of Christ: for it is the power of God unto salvation to every one that believeth; to the Jew first, and also to the Greek*' (KJV). His ministry never neglected his Jewish brethren, as he led many to faith in Jesus, and he was well known for his boldness in Germany and in Russia. A few years later the church of Kurland called him as their missionary to the Jews. This ex-rabbi lived in two worlds. His work among Gentiles was to instil in them a love for God's ancient people, and his work with the Jews was to introduce them to their Messiah. On his deathbed, at the age of 73, his text was Psalm 122:1–3:

> *'I rejoice in those who told me: Let us go into the house of the Lord! Our feet stand in thy gates, Jerusalem. Jerusalem is built to be a city where the people should gather'* (translation unknown).

Rabbi Asher Levy

Asher served as a rabbi for 35 years, after entering theological school at the age of 15 and being ordained in Romania at the age of 21. Success in his ministry did not bring happiness, however, and despite outward appearances he was empty inside.

One day he poured his heart out to a fellow Jew, not knowing that his confidant was a believer in Jesus. His advice was to read Isaiah 53, and this stirred Asher on a voyage of discovery through the Hebrew scriptures. He read:

> *'He was wounded for our transgressions, he was bruised for our iniquities'* (Is. 53:5, KJV).

Isaiah gave another signpost:

> *'For unto us a child is born, unto us a son is given: and the government shall be upon his shoulder: and his name shall be*

called Wonderful, Counsellor, The mighty God, The everlast-
ing Father, The Prince of Peace. Of the increase of his govern-
ment and peace there shall be no end, upon the throne of
David, and upon his kingdom, to order it, and to establish it
with judgment and with justice from henceforth even for ever.
The zeal of the LORD of hosts will perform this' (Is. 9:6–7, KJV).

He also read:

'Hear ye now, O house of David; Is it a small thing for you to
weary men, but will ye weary my God also? Therefore the Lord
himself shall give you a sign; Behold, a virgin shall conceive,
and bear a son, and shall call his name Immanuel' (Is. 7:13–14,
KJV).

Such Old Testament scriptures helped Asher to understand that Jesus was and is the Messiah in whom all the
prophecies were fulfilled. This was confirmed to him
when he had completed his reading of the New
Testament. He came to the conclusion that Jesus of
Nazareth was a Jew of the seed of Abraham and David,
and that he was born of a Jewish virgin in the Jewish
town of Bethlehem, of a Jewish tribe, the tribe of Judah.

Asher was not conscious of following a Saviour of the
Gentiles, but knew him as one for his own people too.
He wrote:

'I feel that I am still a Jew and shall always be a Jew. I have not
renounced our inheritance of Abraham, Isaac and Jacob. Like
Paul, I can say after my acceptance of Christ as my Saviour: "Are
they Hebrews? So am I. Are they Israelites? So am I. Are they the
seed of Abraham? So am I!" (2 Cor. 11:22). Thus, I repeat with
pride the word of Romans 1:16: "For I am not ashamed of the
gospel of Christ, for it is the power of God unto salvation to every
one that believeth; to the Jew first, and also to the Greek."'

Asher still witnesses to these facts as he lives and works today.

Rabbi Max Wertheimer (1863–1941)

Max, too, had an Orthodox Jewish upbringing, brought up in Germany by devout parents, his religious training starting when he was 5. But he fell away while working through an apprenticeship and drifted from the faith of his fathers. His parents sent him to America to knock some sense into him; there he studied at the Hebrew Union College in Cincinnati, Ohio. He immersed himself in Hebrew, Judaism and Jewish history and was eventually ordained as a rabbi in the Reformed tradition, throwing himself into his vocation with passion and great energy.

So confident was he in his faith and calling that he accepted an invitation to speak at a pastors' conference at the Christian Church of Dayton in 1895, where he told them why he was a Jew and would not believe in their Christ as his Messiah and Saviour. His religious views acknowledged no need of an atoning sacrifice for sin; he was guided instead by an ethical religious system. In the audience sat a devout Christian who was deeply stirred as she listened. 'O God,' she prayed, '*bring Dr Wertheimer to realize his utter need of that Saviour he proudly rejects. Bring him, if necessary, to the very depths in order that he may know his need of my Lord, Jesus the Messiah.*'

Life was good for Rabbi Max. An attractive, capable wife, wonderful children, a beautiful home, a comfortable income, a place of prominence in the community, even two servants. Then came a wake-up call. His wife became ill and died and his life unravelled. His dreams shattered, he found himself walking the streets, striving to forget the void in his heart and life. He found himself questioning God, his assurances crumbling. He compared himself to Job, when he cried, *'My days are swifter than a weaver's shuttle, and are spent without hope'* (Job 7:6, KJV).

He resigned as rabbi and dedicated himself to studying his religious heritage. Judaism answered no questions; it satisfied no craving of his heart. Then he opened the New Testament, to compare it with the Hebrew scriptures. One passage screamed at him: Isaiah 53.

> *'By his knowledge shall my righteous servant justify many, for he shall bear their iniquities'* (Is. 53:11, KJV).

He noticed that here was the only mention of the phrase 'My righteous servant' that he could find. It is found nowhere else in the Word of God. We find 'David, my servant', 'Isaiah, my servant' and 'Daniel, my servant', but here was 'My righteous servant'.

Max was determined to identify this 'righteous servant'. He decided that contrary to what he had been taught, it is not Israel, because the prophet declares Israel to be 'a sinful nation', 'a people laden with iniquity', 'a leprous nation'. The righteous servant of Jehovah must be one who is holy. If it isn't Israel, who could it be? He also discarded Isaiah himself in this role ('a man of unclean lips', Is. 6:5) but was led to Isaiah 50:6, where he read, *'I gave my back to the smiters.'* It was God Himself speaking! Max decided to re-read the whole book of Isaiah, but stopped at a verse in chapter 9:

> *'For unto us a child is born, unto us a son is given: and the government shall be upon his shoulder: and his name shall be called Wonderful, Counsellor, The Mighty God, The everlasting Father, The Prince of Peace'* (Is. 9:6, KJV).

The questions continued. The Trinity was next on his list, and Max explored the concept of 'oneness' from a Hebrew perspective. He came to the realization that this was not the stumbling block he had been taught to believe it was. Another question was, 'If he who was crucified was truly an incarnation of God, then who was in heaven?' He received an answer from his reading of the account of Abraham and the three angels in Genesis 18. How and why could there be two 'Gods', one walking the streets of Sodom and another in heaven? It must be one omnipresent God! Then if that were true, He could have been simultaneously in heaven and on the cross.

Max had reached the point of understanding. After months of searching, he was convinced that Jesus was the righteous servant of God (Jehovah Tsidkenu). As he wrote,

> '"The Lord our righteousness!" I cried. "Lord, I believe that Thou as Jehovah Yeshua hast made the atonement for me. I believe that Jehovah Yeshua died for me! I believe Thou hast made provision for me! I believe Thou hast the ability and power! From henceforth I will publicly confess Yeshua as my Saviour and Lord!"'

On 30 March 1904 he publicly confessed Christ in the Central Baptist Church and commenced his new calling as a preacher of the Gospel. He studied at Southern Baptist Seminary in Louisville, Kentucky, and was ordained as a pastor. His first call came from Ada, Ohio, where he was pastor for five years, and he then served at the New Covenant Mission in Pittsburgh. After two-and-a-half years of this ministry, he was convinced that God was calling him to preach to both Jew and Gentile, depending upon the Lord for the support of his family.

Today's attitudes

But what about now? How is Jesus viewed by the Jewish community in general? In the main he is ignored as an irrelevance: an attitude shared with the majority of people in our secularized western society. Ironically, the Muslims have a higher view of this first-century Jew than do those of his own race, as they see him as a (minor) prophet. The only Jews with a real opinion are those who consider themselves religious and those concerned with deciding who is allowed to immigrate into Israel. The opinion in both cases is decidedly negative, yet there are positive murmurings in the sea of indignation.

Some higher educational establishments in Israel, as well as some Jewish colleges elsewhere, are looking at the New Testament as a historical source. Jewish scholars of international repute, Geza Vermes, C.G. Montefiore, Joseph Klausner, Dan Cohn-Sherbok, Pinchas Lapide and David Flusser, have written books about Jesus. In his opening pages Vermes declared his intention to be '*to discover the authentic, original, historical meaning of the words and events reported in the Gospels*'. Klausner's book *Jesus of Nazareth* is probably the most influential book yet written on Jesus by a Jewish non-believer. In the introduction he stated that his book would be the first Hebrew book about Jesus that neither attempted to convert Jews to Christianity nor attempted to make Christianity obnoxious to Jews. He expected, as a consequence, that this book would be equally hated by Jews and Christians!

Modern Jewish scholars are seeking for the Jesus of history, not the Christ of Christianity. They wish to reclaim Jesus the Jew without considering his Messianic claims. They are happy to research the possibility that

Jesus may have been a Pharisee, a zealot or even a prophet, but are not so willing to investigate his claims as Messiah, Son of God or Son of Man. Well, not yet anyway. Perhaps it's stretching it a bit for them to consider Jesus a *Haver*, but at least they are talking about him. Who knows what the future may hold?

11

Mashiach ben David

*Question: Who is going to be really surprised
when Jesus returns?*

How often have you heard someone say, 'I've got Jesus
in my heart'? Metaphorically speaking it may be so, but
reality is so different, because when Jesus left this earth
for heaven, it was the Holy Spirit who took his place and
who lives in the hearts of believers.

So if Jesus is not in our hearts, where in heaven is he
now? That's exactly where he is, and he has been there
since his ascension.

> 'After he said this, he was taken up before their very eyes, and a
> cloud hid him from their sight. They were looking intently up
> into the sky as he was going, when suddenly two men dressed
> in white stood beside them. "Men of Galilee," they said, "why
> do you stand here looking into the sky? This same Jesus, who
> has been taken from you into heaven, will come back in the same
> way you have seen him go into heaven"' (Acts 1:9–11).

So Jesus is in heaven. He is on his throne, at the right
hand of God the Father. He's not whiling away his time

contemplating his navel; he's busier now than he's ever been. He is interceding for us before God. He is our heavenly advocate, just as the devil is our accuser. And as none of us is perfect, there's a real battle going on over us. But there will be an end to it one day. Jesus is waiting for *the* big day. He's ready to get dressed up for his return.

> *'And when I turned I saw seven golden lampstands, and among the lampstands was someone "like a son of man", dressed in a robe reaching down to his feet and with a golden sash round his chest. His head and hair were white like wool, as white as snow, and his eyes were like blazing fire. His feet were like bronze glowing in a furnace, and his voice was like the sound of rushing waters. In his right hand he held seven stars, and out of his mouth came a sharp double-edged sword. His face was like the sun shining in all its brilliance'* (Rev. 1:12–16).

One like a son of man, eh? Where have we heard that before? Well, the above is an allusion to Daniel 7:13–14:

> *'In my vision at night I looked, and there before me was one like a son of man, coming with the clouds of heaven. He approached the Ancient of Days and was led into his presence. He was given authority, glory and sovereign power; all peoples, nations and men of every language worshipped him. His dominion is an everlasting dominion that will not pass away, and his kingdom is one that will never be destroyed.'*

Of course, as we have already read, when Jesus first came to the earth he identified in no uncertain terms with this supernatural figure, but he always said that his time to reveal himself completely in this role had not yet come:

'For as lightning that comes from the east is visible even in the west, so will be the coming of the Son of Man' (Mt. 24:27).

'At that time the sign of the Son of Man will appear in the sky, and all the nations of the earth will mourn. They will see the Son of Man coming on the clouds of the sky, with power and great glory' (Mt. 24:30).

'When the Son of Man comes in his glory, and all the angels with him, he will sit on his throne in heavenly glory' (Mt. 25:31).

This is the Christian view, the Second Coming of Jesus Christ. But what is the Jewish expectation? To find out we have to return to the aftermath of Jesus' first visit to earth.

There are mistakes and then there are *big* mistakes. A small mistake would be forgetting someone's birthday; a big mistake would be if that person was the wife or mother! A small mistake would be failing to recognize an old friend at a party; a big mistake would be if he was the host of the party! A bigger mistake would be failing to recognize the promised saviour of your people, despite him ticking all the right boxes; but the *biggest* mistake of all would be to cover up your mistake and make it near impossible for your people to have a chance to decide for themselves. This is a mistake of the nth degree. I even went so far as to state earlier that this was probably the biggest mistake ever made by any people group in the history of the world.

The Jewish leadership's failure to recognize Jesus as Messiah two thousand years ago was a tragedy comparable to the Holocaust, because it initiated a divine timetable (for more of this read *The Land of Many Names*) that dictated a sorrowful and painful history, paving the way not just for the catastrophes of the mid-twentieth century but for the current isolation of the nation of Israel and the precarious existence of Jewish people worldwide.

We can have justified sympathy for Jewish people, particularly for their religious leadership, on account of their incredible history and their role in the great divine narrative in producing the environment and background for the coming of the Messiah of the world. We can sympathize further when we investigate the shameful treatment the Jewish people have suffered at the hands of the Christian church over the past fifteen centuries. We can stand amazed when we consider how much these people have put up with at the hands of others, yet they have defeated all the odds, survived and even flourished, contributing more to humankind proportionally than any other people group, despite being misunderstood and even hated by most of the other people groups.

But in the most important matters of all, those of personal and corporate redemption, they have been their own worst enemies. And it's all down to the biggest mistake they have ever made, the smokescreen they have created to obscure the identity of the Messiah who came into the world to offer them salvation at a time when the rest of the world was following cunningly disguised spirits from the pit of hell. Before we consider this, there is one more point to make.

To a Martian, visiting us to observe our ways, it would seem that everyone was a friend of Jesus. Not having a grasp of the nuances of blasphemy, they would hear one name spoken more than any other. Not just by Christians in an attitude of worship, but also by others in an attitude of surprise, shock, anger or frustration! For most, 'Jesus!' or 'Jesus Christ!' or 'Christ!', usually combined with more fruity language, is just a handy exclamation. Not so for Jewish people, though. You rarely hear these words freely spoken by a Jew, even as a casual curse. There's something in the Jewish psyche that filters out and blocks that particular name. What a great job the devil has done!

> *'Everyone who calls on the name of the Lord will be saved'* (Rom. 10:13).

Jewish people have an extra barrier to cross before they can come to the point of faith in the true Messiah. For them, Jesus, the name of the Lord, is not just a swear word but a *curse* word, in the fullest definition of the word. And as for 'Christ', no other word sends such a shiver down a Jewish spine! There's a simple reason for how this can be, and it is laid firmly at the feet of the church. To give you an insight, here are the words that a medieval Jew had to recite when he agreed to convert to Catholicism:

> *'I do here and now renounce every rite and observance of the Jewish religion, detesting all its most solemn ceremonies . . . I promise that I will never return to the vomit of Jewish superstition . . . I will shun all intercourse with other Jews and have the circle of my friends only among other Christians . . . We will not associate with the accursed Jews who remain unbaptized . . . We will not celebrate the Passover, the Sabbath or other feast days connected with the Jewish religion . . . And I absolutely renounce every custom and institution of the Jewish laws . . . In one word I renounce absolutely everything Jewish . . . Together with the ancients, I anathemize also the Chief Rabbis and new evil doctors of the Jews . . .'*[1]

So, an aversion to Jesus is in Jewish genes. Paul foreknew this: he wrote it in his letter to the Romans:

'Israel has experienced a hardening in part . . .' (Rom. 11:25).

But the rabbis have also played their role in this. It's back to the big mistake, the blatant concealing of the identity of the Jewish Messiah. Instead, they look for him elsewhere.

It is one of the thirteen fundamental Jewish Principles of faith:

> *'I believe with complete faith in the coming of Messiah. Though he tarry, nonetheless I await him every day, that he will come.'*

The concept of Messiah has been re-evaluated and repackaged by them in the light of the rejection of Jesus. Here's how it goes . . .

Life on earth is a struggle and things will only get better when the world reaches a state of perfection. This will only happen when the Jewish nation reaches a state of perfection, which – let's be frank – is not going to happen. This is where the Messiah comes in. Here will be a man, descended from King David, who will nudge the Jews to their destiny and bring peace to the world. He will bring the Jews back to Israel, rebuild the holy temple, abolish anti-Semitism and act as Israel's teacher and spiritual mentor. The earthly model for this role was Moses, the first redeemer of the Jewish people.

The identity of the Messiah is an easy one. If someone comes along and does all the things that the Messiah was meant to do, then that's who he is; he will be known by his works. If someone comes along and just does 99 per cent of the right stuff, then he's an impostor and the Jews go on looking and longing for Messiah. And this brings us nicely to the question of Jesus.

For the rabbis it's a no-brainer. Did Jesus fulfil all the things that the Messiah was meant to, in the eyes of the rabbis? Well, we examined this in an earlier chapter and the answer was definitely 'No!' Yet religious Jews give the simplest of instructions to those 'targeted by missionaries'. They are told just to walk away and not to get into 'fruitless discussion', because no way can Jesus be the Messiah – he definitely hasn't banished war (Christians have certainly started more than their fair share), he didn't return Jews to Israel (quite the reverse, they would say), he didn't rebuild the temple, he certainly didn't eradicate anti-Semitism (again, the reverse is true) and was not generally accepted as Israel's teacher. *'Just walk away!'* they cry. *'Walk away from these people. We know he's not our Messiah. My rabbi told me so.'*

My rabbi told me so? So where did *they* hear it from? Who gave them the authority? There are two answers to this. First, and correctly, there's the Word of God, in the Tanakh, the Hebrew scriptures. Secondly, it's other rabbis, ancient rabbis from the pages of Jewish history. It is worth now differentiating between these two answers and looking at how they apply the source material, especially when it is coming from the Word of God.

Now we have already looked at the Jewish expectation of the Messiah in the Tanakh, the Old Testament. We identified the Suffering Servant that the Tanakh speaks of. This is the individual identified by Christians as Jesus in his incarnation in the first century. Then we met a new figure, the Messiah Son of Joseph, created by the rabbis as an attempt to fulfil those scriptures that Jesus fits so well. This leads us to the main man, the one they are still waiting for, the king, the Messiah Son of David, or simply Messiah. He is mentioned a lot in the Tanakh. Here are a few examples:

> *'In the last days the mountain of the LORD's temple will be established as chief among the mountains; it will be raised*

above the hills, and all nations will stream to it. Many peoples will come and say, "Come, let us go up to the mountain of the LORD, *to the house of the God of Jacob. He will teach us his ways, so that we may walk in his paths." The law will go out from Zion, the word of the* LORD *from Jerusalem. He will judge between the nations and will settle disputes for many peoples. They will beat their swords into ploughshares and their spears into pruning hooks. Nation will not take up sword against nation, nor will they train for war any more'* (Is. 2:2–4).

'See, the LORD *is coming with fire, and his chariots are like a whirlwind; he will bring down his anger with fury, and his rebuke with flames of fire. For with fire and with his sword the* LORD *will execute judgment upon all men, and many will be those slain by the* LORD*'* (Is. 66:15–16).

'On that day his feet will stand on the Mount of Olives, east of Jerusalem, and the Mount of Olives will be split in two from east to west, forming a great valley, with half of the mountain moving north and half moving south. You will flee by my mountain valley, for it will extend to Azel. You will flee as you fled from the earthquake in the days of Uzziah king of Judah. Then the LORD *my God will come, and all the holy ones with him. On that day there will be no light, no cold or frost. It will be a unique day, without daytime or night-time – a day known to the* LORD. *When evening comes, there will be light. On that day living water will flow out from Jerusalem, half to the eastern sea and half to the western sea, in summer and in winter. The* LORD *will be king over the whole earth. On that day there will be one* LORD, *and his name the only name'* (Zech. 14:4–9).

This promised one is called the Messiah son of David, because he is expected to be descended from King David, as God promised the king through the words of Nathan the prophet:

*'When your days are over and you go to be with your fathers,
I will raise up your offspring to succeed you, one of your own
sons, and I will establish his kingdom. He is the one who will
build a house for me, and I will establish his throne for ever. I
will be his father, and he will be my son. I will never take my
love away from him, as I took it away from your predecessor. I
will set him over my house and my kingdom for ever; his
throne will be established for ever' (1 Chron. 17:11–14).*

This would be the Messiah's earthly calling card, his
necessary pedigree. This is why the genealogies feature
so strongly in the Gospels – if Jesus couldn't prove his
royal lineage, his whole ministry and calling would be
invalid. So this Messiah for whom the Jews are waiting
must also be able to show his pedigree.

Problem. How on earth can anyone show a genealogy
that stretches back around three thousand years? Even
our Royal Family can't go back that far, let alone a people who have rarely stayed in one place for more than
two or three generations! Another problem is that as all
family records were kept in the Jerusalem temple, no
one coming after the destruction of the temple by the
Romans in AD 70 would ever be able to prove his ances-
try beyond a shadow of a doubt. Unless, of course, the
Messiah came before AD 70!

So the Messiah, Son of David, the Jews are still waiting for should really be the Messiah, possibly-but-could-
never-be-absolutely-sure son of David. Nevertheless
they still wait. And, as we already have discovered,
there is a curious slant to this waiting.

There are two possible ways that the Messiah can
come. Either he will come when he is ordained to come,
or his coming can be speeded up if the Jewish people
voluntarily repent. So there are two paths to the
Messiah. If the Jewish people repent, the coming of the

Messiah will be a miraculous and wonderful event; otherwise it will be 'mundane', a natural historic process.

To remind you, these two 'comings' are their way of explaining whether the Messiah will come as the 'Son of Joseph' or the 'Son of David'. The 'mundane' coming, which will kick in if there is no Jewish repentance, will be the 'Son of Joseph'. So what they are saying is that if the Jews do not repent, they are going to get the 'Son of Joseph' first. It's almost as if there is an implied threat here to the Jewish people that unless they get their act together, they are going to get the *inferior* Messiah and not the 'all conquering king' who is going to bang heads together and sort out the nations. Get on your knees and let's usher in the Arnie Schwarzemessiah!

So, if they don't repent first, they will get this one . . .

> 'Rejoice greatly, O Daughter of Zion! Shout, Daughter of Jerusalem! See, your king comes to you, righteous and having salvation, gentle and riding on a donkey, on a colt, the foal of a donkey' (Zech. 9:9).

And if they do repent first, they will get this one . . .

> 'In my vision at night I looked, and there before me was one like a son of man, coming with the clouds of heaven. He approached the Ancient of Days and was led into his presence' (Dan. 7:13).

What about the holy temple? If they don't repent first, the Messiah will organize the rebuilding of the temple, but if they do repent first, the temple will drop from heaven, fully built!

If, when you are visiting New York, a van pulls up and to the accompaniment of oriental melodies blaring out through huge speakers on the roof you are accosted by wiry, curly-haired men in black, you are not being mugged or abducted into the mother ship. No, you have met some Lubavitcher Jews and their 'Mitzvah Tank'. You are spared embarrassment if you answer in the negative to the first question, 'Are you Jewish?' Otherwise you are coaxed into the van to put on *tefillin*. You will roll up your left sleeve, bind the ceremonial paraphernalia to your arm and recite a prayer. At least it is less painful than giving blood! You will then be given a small kit to instruct you on how to light Sabbath candles and further literature as their way of saying thanks for the *mitzvah* you have made, doing your little bit to usher in the *Mashiach* (Messiah). The mitzvah, the divine instruction, is your good deed, not quite the fully blown repentance that would have been preferred, but not to be sneezed at. This concept of public good deeds was dreamt up by their rabbi, the now deceased *Lubavitcher Rebbe*, Menachem Schneerson, who, until he died in 1994, was the odds-on favourite Messiah candidate of his generation. He said:

> *'A mitzvah is a deed of cosmic significance, a deed of infinite value unto itself.'*

His belief was that just one person performing a single mitzvah could be performing the very deed that tips the scales, ushers in the Messiah and brings redemption to the world. Yes, in the words of the Lottery operators, it could be you!

Well, anyway, that's how they see the whole Messiah thing. What's really going to happen is the following (as excerpted from *The Land of Many Names*), looking forward to the day when Jesus, the true Son of David, *Mashiach ben David*, makes his final appearance.

What an awesome day that will be. God will show His power, stronger than any Cruise or Scud missile, and the whole world is going to realize what a terrible mistake it has made in turning its back on the one true God. The Jewish people will particularly be affected as the truth finally dawns on them. Their reaction to this knowledge will be significant. We read in Zechariah 12:10:

> *'And I will pour out on the house of David and the inhabitants of Jerusalem a spirit of grace and supplication. They will look on me, the one they have pierced, and they will mourn for him as one mourns for an only child and grieve bitterly for him as one grieves for a first-born son.'*

The awful realization of the identity of Jesus their Messiah, the *'one they had pierced'*, will initiate a national repentance the like of which the world has never seen before. The next three verses bear testimony to this, speaking of every clan in the land weeping and mourning. Then, perhaps led by their religious leaders, Orthodox and Messianic believers together (though, of course, all will now be 'Messianic'), they will sing the Messianic Psalm, Psalm 118, as Matthew 23:39 tells us, *'For I tell you, you will not see me again until you say, "Blessed is he who comes in the name of the Lord,"'* and the Lord Jesus will return.

And where will he return? Certainly not in the world capitals of London, Paris or Washington. A clue is given in Acts, chapter 1. The scene is the Mount of Olives, overlooking Jerusalem on the east side. Jesus is with his disciples for one last time, when suddenly a cloud hides him from their sight and he is taken back into heaven. The angel's last words to them are in verse 11:

> *'This same Jesus, who has been taken from you into heaven, will come back in the same way you have seen him go into heaven.'*

He is going to return in the same way that he went – from heaven to the Mount of Olives. If you complain that I'm reading too much into the text, then head to Zechariah, chapter 14. We read another account of that final battle over Jerusalem. More depressing details are given but again we are told that it is God Himself, or specifically the Messiah, who will fight against these armies of the nations. In fact it's the first thing he does when he returns. Verse 4 tells us:

> *'On that day his feet will stand on the Mount of Olives, east of Jerusalem, and the Mount of Olives will be split in two from east to west, forming a great valley, with half of the mountain moving north and half moving south.'*

It is going to be a truly awesome sight and the very geography of the region is going to be altered as a result. The Mount of Olives will be split in two and we read of a great river forming, flowing from east to west.

Jesus will return as Messiah King. No longer the Suffering Servant of his first coming. This time he will come to reign among his people, as the Son of David. He will come to live out those Old Testament scriptures that were not fulfilled by his first coming. For example, Isaiah 2:3–4:

> *'Many peoples will come and say, "Come, let us go up to the mountain of the LORD, to the house of the God of Jacob. He will teach us his ways, so that we may walk in his paths." The law will go out from Zion, the word of the LORD from Jerusalem. He will judge between the nations and will settle disputes for many peoples. They will beat their swords into ploughshares and their spears into pruning hooks. Nation will not take up sword against nation, nor will they train for war any more.'*

Come, Lord Jesus.

Notes

[1] Michael Brown, *Our Hands are Stained with Blood* (Destiny Image, 1992), p. 95–96.

PART FOUR

Eternity and Antiquity

12

The Man of Many Names

*Question: How can we unify all of these portraits
of Jesus into one image?*

*'I am a Jew, but I am enthralled by the luminous figure of the
Nazarene. Jesus is too colossal for the pen of phrasemongers,
however artful. No man can read the Gospels without feeling
the actual presence of Jesus. His personality pulsates in every
word. No myth is filled with such life.' (Albert Einstein)*

If this admission is from an unbeliever who never
acknowledged Jesus as Saviour, how can those of us who
do accept him as Lord express ourselves adequately? The
truth is that we can't: he is just 'too colossal for the pen of
phrasemongers'. We can only scratch around in our limited human capacity and marvel at the fact that he actually cares about us and bothers with us.

He who set the planets in their orbit, who planted the
trees, plotted the paths of the winds and programmed
Adam's DNA in that garden of paradise is also the one
who will return to a battered, abused world and judge
the billions of souls, most of them terrified and regretful.
He is the bridge of the ages, present at the beginning, at

the end and at all points in between. He created us, he teaches us, he redeems us. He provides a hope for the future and offers us help in tackling the present. He is the Man of Many Names, as well as the God of the universe. He is the One.

My hope is that this book has provided you with a rounded view of the Man of Many Names, not just the usual snapshots of his life and ministry in the first century. Thanks to the material provided by the Aramaic Targums, you will now appreciate how involved he was, as the *Memra*, at the time of Creation and how he personally intervened at key moments of Jewish history in his guise of the Angel of the LORD.

It's easy for us to blindly accept the Messianic prophecies in the Old Testament and say, 'Ah yes, that speaks of Jesus: how can they have missed it?' Hindsight is a wonderful thing, but it should never breed complacency and arrogance. The fact is that it's easier for us to look back through the lenses provided by two thousand years of Christian scholarship than to live through those times, with their unique hardships and disadvantages, and come to the same conclusions. No one knows their scriptures better than the Jews themselves, yet they still get it wrong, despite their own two-thousand-year-old cultural lenses.

By spending time analysing their objections to those prophecies that we say speak of Jesus, we have engaged in the key battles and, I believe, have gained new understandings of such signposts as Daniel's seventy weeks and the Suffering Servant passages of Isaiah. If we can overcome the key objections of the Jewish scholars, this can only feed our faith. Of course, as in every battlefield, whether over the Hebrew scriptures or with the atheists in the Creation/Evolution debate, there will always be clever people with clever ideas who will tie you up in knots with their cleverness. The point is that without the illumination in their heart provided by the Holy Spirit, they are never going to get it and will often fight tooth and nail to make sure that others are drawn into their arrogant views. All we can do is speak the truth with love and pray that the Lord will intervene. Hopefully, with the illumination provided by Jewish scholarship, you now have more tools in your armoury to fight the good fight in terms of the authenticity of Jesus' claim to be *The Promised One*.

Of course, most of you were already fully aware of the Jewishness of Jesus, *Yeshua ben Yosef*, but it's still worth reminding ourselves of this, particularly by demonstrating the continuity between the 'Old' and 'New' Testaments and showing the points of similarity between Jesus and Moses. Also it helps to emphasize his humanity, the fact that he walked this earth as a flesh-and-blood human being, despite his divine nature. It was incredible to see how heresies could arise, and we wonder if it would have been far less complicated for the early church if it had retained its Jewish roots and not taken on the pagan, unbiblical views of the Greek world of that day.

Now the usual epithet we use for Jesus is *Christ*: not, as some suppose, his surname, but his Messianic title. By exploring the precise meaning of the 'anointed one' that it refers to, we examined exactly how Jesus fulfilled this role. He set out to demonstrate beyond a shadow of doubt, through miraculous signs, that he was the Christ, the Messiah. Until the religious authorities hatched their nefarious plan to kill him, the people acknowledged his Messiahship, as we can see from the reception they gave him on Palm Sunday.

But Jesus the *rabbi* also came to teach us, to show us how to live. Most of his teachings are apparent to all and speak to us not just across the centuries but also across the cultural gap between his first-century agricultural setting and our twenty-first-century technological age. Key messages from the heart of God still speak to us and will continue to do so until he returns. They undergird our laws and moral framework, and the fact that these are currently crumbling in our society is because of the ineffectiveness of our current church, not of the one who taught us in the first place. Yet there are subtleties to much of his teachings that have been lost in translation, and there is still more we can learn from him and about him by picking up the tools to unlock these nuances. Hopefully you have now learnt enough to want to go deeper. The booklist in Appendix B will help you in this task.

Then there was the title that Jesus preferred above all, *bar anash*, Son of Man. This identified his supernatural mission and his redemptive purposes and gave a foretaste of his Second Coming. He also identified himself as the Son of God, a title quite familiar to Satan and his demons, and it was this appellation that was to bring his downfall: execution on grounds of blasphemy. Yet it was the key to our salvation, and this was explained.

The Jewish religious leadership had a problem. Not only had Jesus come and fulfilled the scriptures, but also other signs had been provided after his ascension to remind them of what they had missed. Rather than accept their mistake, they devised a cunning plan to explain away those scriptures that Jesus seemed to have fulfilled. They invented the Messiah, Son of Joseph, *Mashiach ben Yosef*, as a stop-gap Saviour and created a mysterious set of scenarios to explain his coming appearance. Yet, by identifying this figure with the biblical figure of Joseph, all they have managed to do is remind us of the similarities between this son of Jacob and Jesus himself.

But it went further. In order to ensure that their people would not be enticed into following Jesus, the early rabbis filled the pages of the Talmud, their key religious manual, with negative images of Jesus, known disrespectfully as *Yeshu HaNotzri*, and with some of the most appalling falsehoods. This led to further persecutions at the hands of the church, and the Talmud managed to get itself banned, burned and doctored. It was a war for the hearts and minds of the Jews, and the biggest casualty of the whole sorry episode was the truth itself.

There were also flesh-and-blood casualties, but their fate had been sealed a long time before. Many sneer at the Jewish people for their 'chosenness', perhaps jealous of their accomplishments in a whole swathe of fields and disciplines, or of their centrality on the world's stage, whether through the Holocaust, the State of Israel or the numerous contrived conspiracies speaking of global Jewish domination. What most people fail to realize is that the Jewish people have indeed been chosen, but it's not a choice that they welcome. It's hard to find much joy in being reviled and persecuted. In fact, if the true nature of their divine selection were ever revealed, most Jews would be struck dumb with shock.

Consider this. Without the Crucifixion (at the hands of the Romans), there would be no substitutionary death and subsequent victory over death. For your salvation, someone had to sentence Jesus to death, in accordance with the divine legal system developed over a period of time. It was the Jews who were the instruments of God not just for the development of this religious legal system but for the death of the Messiah. Blame God for the death of Jesus, not His representatives. Thanks to the key early disciples, Peter and Paul, both acting again as God's instruments, the Gentiles were allowed into the church, bringing the prospect of salvation to the whole world. Both were executed by Gentiles for their efforts. The early church then developed a vengeful theology that earmarked the Jews as a rejected and cursed people, responsible for the death of Jesus and abandoned for ever by God. This immediately blocked the path of those Jews to eternal salvation, even as their bodies were battered at the hands of those who expected salvation. How on earth could they put their faith in a Messiah whose followers hated them to death? What an unbelievable irony. But it gets worse.

The Jewish religious leadership reacted to this hatred by making it even more impossible for their own people to find eternal salvation. Through their own religious writings they embarked on a campaign of misinformation, hiding the true face of Jesus and his mission. And still the church acted as 'God's avengers', burning and doctoring these writings and stepping up the persecutions even further, as punishment for the (admittedly) negative portrait of Jesus painted in the pages of the Talmud. The effect of this continuous persecution has been a further hardening of the Jewish heart against the name of Jesus. Is there any wonder that modern-day Jews, whatever their religious affiliation, freely accept any worldview and corruption, from Hinduism to New Age cults, but mention the name of Jesus and they run a mile. Jews who believe in Jesus are the only Jews who have every obstacle thrown at them if they try to immigrate to Israel. Is there any wonder? It is irrational, it is spiritual, it is a tragedy beyond belief.

Yet there have been miracles. Not only have Jews embraced Jesus as their Messiah, but even some brought up in Orthodox Judaism, trained in the Talmud, some as religious leaders for their people. Some have been able to refer to Jesus as *Haver*, friend. Some, such as Alfred Edersheim, David Baron and Arnold Fruchtenbaum, have blessed the church immeasurably with their unique insights. It is worth repeating the verse from Romans:

> *'Again I ask: Did they stumble so as to fall beyond recovery? Not at all! Rather, because of their transgression, salvation has come to the Gentiles to make Israel envious. But if their transgression means riches for the world, and their loss means riches for the Gentiles, how much greater riches will their fullness bring!' (Rom. 11:11–12).*

Finally, Jesus will return as King, Messiah, Son of David, Mashiach ben David. We wait for this day with bated breath.

The Man of Many Names sits in a plush reception area, flanked by fresh flowers and a water cooler. He has come for an interview. He wants to be Lord of your heart and your mind, but first needs an invitation. This you have given, and he has come willingly for an interview, a personal encounter with you. Those who call themselves Christians have had this personal experience of meeting with the Master and have extended the experience beyond this initial encounter through the privilege of prayer. For many of us, this first interview has secured the position. We call it faith, and a personal encounter with Jesus Christ is often sufficient to seal the deal.

But to continue with our job interview parallel, in the cut-throat business world the interview is just part of the process and most don't even get that far. The crucial element is the CV, the Curriculum Vitae. This is the document sent to the employer, in which all aspects of the applicant's life are laid bare. The CV gives details of the background, training, skills and aspirations. It is a holistic snapshot of the applicant, providing enough information for a decision on whether the application is to be taken further.

I have attempted in this book to provide a CV for Jesus, the Man of Many Names. We have his name, in fact a dozen or so of his main ones. We also have both his current address (heaven) and a full employment history, past and future, from the dawn of time to the end of days. A complete list of skills and attributes is furnished for him as God's communicator to humankind, teacher, healer, prophet, priest and king. His achievements are laid out, not the least being the work done on the cross to redeem us and provide us with eternal life in his presence. As for references, a million testimonies of redeemed lives bear witness to his character, with those folk in Chapter 10 as starters.

It is our responsibility to have a good read of this CV, to find out as much as we can about the One we have surrendered our life to. The heart may be won over, but the brain also needs to be engaged. Jesus, Son of Man, Son of God, Rabbi and Christ, all titles and pieces of the mosaic that fit together to provide the perfect portrait of the Man of Many Names. Understanding these titles is to understand the Man and his mission. I pray that this book will have filled in a few gaps in your understanding and encouraged you to dig deeper.

Let's face it, who could refuse this man an interview on the back of such a pedigree and glowing record of achievement? If he's sitting in your reception area waiting for a personal encounter, what are you waiting for?

APPENDICES

Appendix A

The Traditions of the Elders

It will not have escaped your attention that many Jewish writings have been referenced in this book. It's probably been a bit confusing, so here is a description of all such writings to help you in your understanding. But first, a controversy.

Orthodox Judaism states that when Moses was receiving the Law on Mount Sinai, he first received the *written* Torah, the words that would become the Holy Scripture of the first five books of the Bible. But that wasn't the whole story, they tell us, because then came the *oral* Torah, the words that would not be written down but would become the *commentary* on the scriptures. Poor old Moses, so much to remember – even the written Torah wouldn't be committed to parchment for another forty years or so!

In the view of the Orthodox Jews, the oral Torah is key, as it explains how we should interpret the scriptures. The written Torah is just the raw material, the shell from which to extract the vast teaching of the Torah. The idea seems to be that although the oral Law was given to Moses by God and preserved by being passed down intact from teacher to student, it had to be written down eventually. The reason for this was the turbulence and uncertainty of Jewish life, with expulsions and migrations forced upon them and the loss of a cohesive structured society in one geographical position. If it hadn't been written down it would have been lost.

So around AD 200, Rabbi Judah HaNasi took on the task of writing down the oral Law. He created the *Mishnah* (the 'repetition'), considered the first major work of Judaism since the completion of the Hebrew scriptures. So the Mishnah is basically all the stuff that God gave to Moses on Mount Sinai apart from what ended up in the first five books of the Bible. The sages who were the final generation of custodians of this oral Law were the 120 teachers known as the *Tannaim*, who covered six generations from the destruction of the Jerusalem temple in AD 70 to AD 200, when the Mishnah was compiled.

Over the next four centuries, other sages known as the *Amoraim* took it upon themselves to comment on this written material, adding a vast amount of material as commentary to the Mishnah. Although the Mishnah was written in Hebrew, most of the commentary was written in Aramaic. This became known as the *Gemara* (the 'completion') and the whole lot together became the Talmud. The Gemara was compiled in two separate places, the two great centres of Jewish learning at the time. The first was compiled in Israel, becoming known as the *Jerusalem Talmud*, and the second, the larger volume, was the *Babylonian Talmud*. It was this latter one that became the Talmud of history. The most commonly available Talmud today is the Steinsaltz Talmud, with around two million copies distributed around the world. If you're thinking of adding it to your collection of holy books, think again: this one runs to 39 volumes, so don't expect much change from $1000.

The other main body of literature produced by the Jewish sages was the *Midrash*. These were commentaries, usually on books of the Bible, but also on the Talmud. The first of these were produced at the time of the Amoraim and some were still being written as late as the twelfth century AD. The Midrash used in the early chapters of this book is Genesis Rabbah, which was written between AD 400 and 650.

A little earlier than this was going on, other sages were writing the *Targums*. These were Aramaic translations of the Hebrew Bible and made use of a lot of the techniques found in the *Midrashim* (plural of Midrash). The need for Targums paralleled the current trend for producing versions of the Bible to speak into all sorts of sub-cultures. We have the Cockney Bible, the Manga Bible, even the Glasgow Bible, 'relating some of the biblical tales in the Glaswegian vernacular'. From before the time of Jesus until some time afterwards, the language of the people was not Hebrew but Aramaic, a language brought back by those who returned from exile. Hebrew was the language of the 'Hebrew' scriptures, so when they were read out in synagogues not everyone was able to follow what was going on. The Targums were written to give extra insights into the scriptures, written in the language of the times.

The two main Targums were Onkelos, which commented on the Torah, and Jonathan, which commented on the rest of the Hebrew scriptures.

Appendix B

Recommended Reading

Of course there are thousands of books about Jesus, but here are those that helped me most in my researches and will help you to dig deeper into the subject. To help you further, I have arranged this material by chapter heading, indicating where the book was of most use.

Memra
The Messiah Texts, Raphael Patai, Wayne State University Press, 1988
The Talmud, H. Polano, The Book Tree, 2003
The Legends of the Jews, Louis Ginzberg, Johns Hopkins University Press, 1998

The Angel of the LORD
The Messiah in the Old Testament, Risto Santala, Keren Ahvah Meshihit, 1992

The Promised One
Messiah: His Nature and Person, David L. Cooper, 1933
Rays of Messiah's Glory, David Baron, Messianic Testimony, 2000

What the Rabbis know about the Messiah, Rachmiel Frydland, Messianic Publishing Company, 1985

Yeshua ben Yosef
Jesus was a Jew, Arnold Fruchtenbaum, Ariel Ministries, 1981
Jesus ben Joseph, Walter Riggans, Monarch, 1993
The Messiah in the New Testament, Risto Santala, Keren Ahvah Meshihit, 1992

Christ
Unlocking the Bible, David Pawson, Collins, 2001

Rabbi
Roots and Branches, David Bivin et al, PWM Trust, 1998
Yeshua, Dr Ron Moseley, Lederer Books, 1996

Bar Anash
Jesus the Jewish Theologian, Brad H. Young, Hendrickson, 1995

Mashiach ben Yosef
The Messiah Factor, Tony Pearce, New Wine, 2004
Final Words of Jesus, Jacob Prasch, MSP, 1999

Yeshu HaNotzri
Our Father Abraham, Marvin R. Wilson, Eerdmans, 1991
Jesus of Nazareth, Joseph Klausner, Menorah Publishing Company, 1979

Haver
The Messiahship of Jesus, Arthur W. Kac, Moody Press, 1981
The Jewish Reclamation of Jesus, Donald Hagner, Wipf and Stock, 1997

Mashiach ben David
Yeshua ben David, Walter Riggans, Monarch, 1995
Where is Jesus Now?, David Pawson, Kingsway, 2001

Appendix C

Glossary of Jewish Terms

For some, the odd word or two is decidedly odd and unfamiliar. Here is a brief description of Jewish terms used in this book that should help you overcome this.

Allusion
A teaching method used by Jesus that encourages the listener to make connections between scriptures and come to a natural conclusion.

Almah
Hebrew word translated as 'virgin', most notably in Isaiah 7:14.

Amidah
The central prayer of the Jewish liturgy. It literally translates as 'standing'. It consists of nineteen separate blessings.

Angel of the Lord
A supernatural being who appears at key times throughout the Old Testament (Hebrew scriptures, Tanakh).

Ani maamin
A collection of the thirteen principles of faith, written by the Jewish sage Maimonides.

Anointed One
Individual identified in the Old Testament (Hebrew scriptures, Tanakh) as the Promised One. Hebrew word is *Mashiach*, transliterated as the English word 'Messiah'.

Aramaic
Middle Eastern language introduced to Israel by the Assyrian invaders at the time of the kings and also by Jews returning after Babylonian captivity. It is the language of much of the book of Daniel, and some Aramaic phrases appear in the Gospels.

Atnach
A mark on the original Hebrew text produced by the Masoretes, said to be for punctuation or musical purposes.

Baba mezia
A part (tractate) of the Babylonian Talmud.

Bar anash
Aramaic phrase translated 'Son of Man' in Daniel 7:13–14.

Birkat HaMinim
The twelfth prayer or benediction in the Amidah. It asks God to destroy those in heretical sects, with particular relevance to Jews who had decided to follow Jesus.

Christ
The English translation of the Greek word *Christos*, which itself is the New Testament translation of the Hebrew word *Mashiach*, meaning 'Anointed One'.

Day of Atonement
See Yom Kippur.

Emmanuel
A name of the future Messiah taken from Isaiah 7:14. It literally means 'God with us'.

Feast of Tabernacles
See Succot.

Gemara
The part of the Talmud that contains the commentaries on the Mishnah. It is an Aramaic word meaning 'tradition'.

Genesis Rabbah
A Midrash containing commentaries on the book of Genesis. Also known as 'Bereshit Rabbah'.

Haftarah
This is scripture, taken from the prophetic books (Nevi'im), that is read after the Torah portions every Sabbath in the synagogues.

Haver
Hebrew for 'friend'.

Hebrew scriptures
The Jewish Bible, equivalent to the Christian Bible's Old Testament, but with the books arranged in a different order. See Tanakh.

Immanuel
See Emmanuel.

Jesus
The English transliteration of the Greek word *Iesous* found in the New Testament, itself a transliteration of the Hebrew word *Yeshua*, his given name.

Kal vachomer
A teaching technique used by Jesus and the rabbis to determine something more obvious from something less obvious.

Ketuvim
The third part of the Tanakh (Hebrew scriptures), containing the 'writings'.

Maimonides
A highly influential Jewish rabbi from Spain in the twelfth century AD. His full name was Moses ben Maimon and he was also known as the Rambam.

Mashiach
Hebrew word from Hebrew scriptures translated as 'the Anointed One' and transliterated into English as 'Messiah'.

Masoretes
A group of Jewish scribes working between the seventh and eleventh centuries to make the text of the Hebrew scriptures (Tanakh) more accessible by adding punctuation and verse divisions.

Masoretic text
The text of the Hebrew scriptures (Tanakh) used by Jews. It was created by the Masoretes.

Memra
Aramaic word that is the equivalent to the Greek word *logos*, used in John 1:1. It is translated 'word'.

Meshuggenah
Yiddish word meaning 'madman'.

Meshumed
Hebrew word for an 'apostate', a Jew who has become a follower of Jesus.

Messiah
English transliteration of the Hebrew word *Mashiach* in the Hebrew scriptures, meaning 'the Anointed One'.

Messiah, son of David
The Messiah as awaited by religious Jews, also known simply as the Messiah or Mashiach. He is the kingly conquering figure who will return the Jews to Israel, rebuild the temple and bring an end to wars.

Messiah, son of Joseph
Also known as *Mashiach ben Yosef*. An expectation of rabbinic Judaism: a secondary Messianic figure who will come before the main one, the Messiah, son of David.

Midrash
(Plural *Midrashim*.) Commentaries on the Hebrew scriptures (Tanakh) compiled from the second century onwards.

Minim
Hebrew word referring to Jews who are considered outsiders from their own community.

Miriam
The Hebrew name translated as 'Mary'.

Mishnah
The body of literature created from the second century onwards, a written version of the Jewish oral Law handed down from generation to generation. These were eventually combined with the Gemara to form the Talmud.

Mitzvah
(Plural *Mitzvot*.) Good deeds or commandments (also acts of human kindness). Derived from the 613 mitzvot of the Torah.

Nevi'im
The second part of the Tanakh (Hebrew scriptures), containing the 'prophetic writings'.

Passover
(In Hebrew, *Pesach*.) A Jewish holiday which begins on the fifteenth day of Nisan. It commemorates the Exodus and freedom of the Israelites from ancient Egypt.

Rabbi
Hebrew word for 'teacher' or 'great one', derived from the word *rav*, meaning 'great'.

Rambam
Jewish sage from the twelfth century. His full name was Moses Maimonides (Moses ben Maimon).

Ramban
Jewish sage from the thirteenth century. His full name was Nahmanides.

Rashi
French rabbi from the eleventh century. His full name was Rabbi Shlomo Yitzhaqi. He is famous for the first comprehensive commentaries on the Talmud and the Tanakh.

Sanhedrin
A part (tractate) of the Babylonian Talmud. (Also the great assembly of Jewish judges.)

Septuagint
The Greek version of the Old Testament (Hebrew scriptures), produced in Alexandria in the third to first centuries BC. The name means 'seventy' in Latin.

Shema
Shema Yisrael is the most important prayer in Judaism, taken from Deuteronomy 6:4–9. It translates as 'Hear, O Israel'.

Shiloh
This was the original sanctuary for the Ark of the Covenant until it was taken by the Philistines at the time of the prophet Samuel.

Siddur
This is the prayer book used by Jews throughout the world.

Son of David
This was a title given to the promised Messiah and applied to Jesus in such verses as Matthew 15:22, Matthew 20:30 and Mark 10:47.

Son of God
This is the title often applied to Jesus in the Gospels, though not principally by himself.

Son of Man
This is the title most applied by Jesus to himself. It is taken from Daniel 7:13–14.

Succot
This is a pilgrim festival that occurs on the fifteenth day of the month of Tishri, when the Jews travelled to the temple in Jerusalem at the time of Jesus. It is also known as the Feast of Tabernacles and commemorates the time spent by the ancient Israelites in their desert wanderings, living in booths (Succot).

Suffering Servant
The individual spoken of in Isaiah 53 and identified with Jesus by Christians.

Talmud
The body of Jewish literature created from the second century onwards, comprising the Mishnah (oral Law) and the Gemara (commentaries).

Tanakh
A Hebrew acronym for the Hebrew scriptures. The acronym is taken from the initials of the Torah (Teachings), Nevi'im (Prophets) and Ketuvim (Writings).

Targum
(Plural *Targumim*.) An Aramaic translation of parts of the Hebrew scriptures, dating back at their earliest to Bible times.

Tefillin
Also known as phylacteries, these are two boxes containing Bible verses (from the Torah) which are strapped to the arms and forehead and used in Jewish prayer.

Toledot Yeshu
A medieval Jewish manuscript that claims to give the story of Jesus but is written from an anti-Christian perspective.

Torah
The first part of the Tanakh (Hebrew scriptures), containing the 'teachings'. Also known as the five books of Moses.

Traditions of the Elders
This is the oral Law used by the Pharisees of Jesus' day. It was eventually written down, becoming a part of the Mishnah.

Tzitzit
These are the fringes or tassels on the *tallit* (prayer shawl) of religious Jews.

Yarmulke
Jewish head covering. Also known as 'kippah'.

Yeshu
A name for Jesus in the Talmud. It was an acronym for the Hebrew expression *yemach shemo vezichro*, which means, 'May his name and memory be obliterated.'

Yeshu HaNotzri
A name for Jesus in the Talmud. The second word means 'the Nazarene'.

Yeshua
Jesus' given name in Hebrew.

Yom Kippur
(Day of Atonement.) Probably the most important holiday of the Jewish year, it is a day set aside to atone for the sins of the past year. It occurs on the tenth day of Tishri and was instituted at Leviticus 23:27.

Yosef
The Hebrew name translated as 'Joseph'.

Zohar
Jewish mystical book used in the practice of Kabbalah, a Jewish mystical tradition dating back to Old Testament times.

THE LAND OF MANY NAMES

Steve Maltz

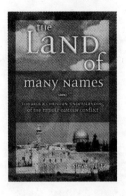

Much heat has been generated by the subject of Israel and Palestine. It's a subject that will not go away and it is crucial that Christians should have a clear grasp of both the spiritual and historical issues involved.

This is a lively, entertaining and provocative introduction to the subject for ordinary Christians. The author takes you on a historical journey of the Land of Many Names, from the Canaan of Abraham to the Promised Land, by way of the Land of Milk and Honey, Israel and Judah, Judea and Samaria, Palestine, The Holy Land, Zion, Israel and 'The Zionist Entity'. At each stage, we pause to consider what God is saying to all concerned and in some places awkward questions are also asked of the reader.

This is an easy read, but it is not a comfortable book.

THE PEOPLE OF MANY NAMES

Steve Maltz

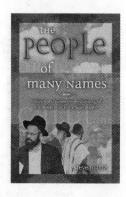

The Jews are a mystery to most, provoking a whole range of questions:

- Who are they? • How have they survived for so long?
- Why have they been so feared or hated by so many people for so many reasons? • What is their relevance to Christians?

This book attempts to give clear answers to these questions and helps the reader to understand the spiritual significance for both Christians and Jews.

This is a lively, entertaining and provocative introduction to the People of Many Names, from early beginnings in the Old Testament as the 'Children of Promise' and a 'Kingdom of Priests', then as the people of 'Galut' (Exile), where they were denigrated as 'Christ killers', 'Dhimmis' and 'Conspirators of Zion'. We view their accomplishments, despite the hostility that surrounded them, including the horrors of the Holocaust, and conclude our story in the New Testament, as the natural branches of God's olive tree.

THE TRUTH IS OUT THERE

Steve Maltz

We love intrigues and mysteries, don't we? Conspiracies are big news. The media industry loves them because we love them, but how much truth do they represent? Don't you want to know what really is going on, who really is pulling the strings in our world today? Wouldn't it be a refreshing change to be presented with the real truth?

Is history just a random sequence of events, or are there secret manipulations? What makes us tick? How did the world as we see it come to be? In this short book we delve below the surface of our existence on this planet, glimpse the possibilities beyond the daily routines of just getting on with life. The conspiracy we uncover has tentacles in all spheres of human life, so where it leads we will follow. We will be taken into areas of science, history, human behaviour, popular culture, religion and little green men. Read this book if you are prepared to be challenged.